The Chinese Puzzle

THE CHINESE PUZZLE

Harriet Graham

Houghton Mifflin Company
Boston 1988

Library of Congress Cataloging-in-Publication Data

Graham, Harriet.
  The Chinese puzzle.

  Reprint. Originally published: London : André
Deutsch, 1987. ꞌS ep.
  Summary: In London of the 1890s, two children
set out to find their guardian who has disappeared
along with his friend, a master magician, and find
themselves captive in an opium den with very dangerous
characters.
  [1. Mystery and detective stories. 2. London
(England)—Fiction] I. Title.
PZ7.G75169Ch   1988   [Fic]   88-6771
ISBN 0-395-47689-5

Published in the United States by Houghton Mifflin Company.
Originally published in Great Britain in 1987 /০ ৭
by André Deutsch Limited, 105-106 Great Russel Street,
London WC1B 3LJ.

Printed in the United States of America

P   10   9   8   7   6   5   4   3   2   1

For B.R.B. Dillon-Weston
In gratitude

CONTENTS

The Chinese Puzzle

PROLOGUE

Sometime during the Spring of 1893 a Chinese boy carrying a canvas bag slung over one shoulder climbed the steep path that led to the house with the red shutters and pushed open the gate. The house stood somewhat apart from the other fine merchants' houses on top of the hill, overlooking Shanghai harbour, and the view from the gardens was said to be the best in the neighbourhood. But the boy didn't linger. He was superstitious, and there was something mysterious about the house with the red shutters; something that made him afraid. So he pushed the newspaper that he was delivering through the railings of the verandah and ran quickly back down the path again without once turning round.

The newspaper lay where the boy had put it until the evening, when the man who owned the house came back and picked it up. After he had finished his evening meal and dismissed the servants, the man sat down beside the window, watching the twinkling lights of the harbour below him and turning the pages of the weekly edition of the *Shanghai Times*. He was a tall man, with a sallow complexion and deep sunk eyes that were neither blue nor brown, but a strange, glittering grey. It was only when he had finished reading the paper and was about to put it back on the table that his attention was suddenly caught by a notice on the back page. He read it through, carefully, several times, and his grey eyes narrowed as he sat back in his chair and gazed once again towards the lights of the harbour. For a long time he stayed there, motionless and deep in thought until at last a slow smile twitched at the corners of his mouth. He began to drum his fingers gently on the folded newspaper in front of him.

Before going to bed that night he wrote a letter for his servant to deliver the next morning to the offices of the *Shanghai Times*.

CHAPTER ONE

In which there is a meeting of Magicians . . .

The letter must have arrived by the late afternoon post. It certainly hadn't been there when I left at half past two to meet Flora. But it was the first thing I saw as we hurtled through the front door of our house in Kennington at tea time. I think I knew, in that very instant, that something extraordinary was about to happen. Some letters are like that. They seem to carry an air of importance with them, so that you know as soon as you see the envelope, and long before you discover what is inside or who they are from, that the news they bring is momentous. I dropped Flora's shoe bag on the floor and stared at the long, creamy envelope that lay on the hall chair where Nellie had put it. The letter was addressed to Samuel in strange, spiky black writing, and along the top were the words: 'Special Delivery'.

The unexpected always seems to happen when you least expect it, of course, and never when you wish it would, such as in the middle of a Latin lesson, or when you've been sent upstairs to tidy your room, or when you're waiting to go in to the dentist. The arrival of the letter was no exception. You see, all the way home Flora and I had been thinking about the next day, and about our visit to the country. Nellie was taking us to stay with Rose and Arthur. Rose is Nellie's sister, and she and her husband, Arthur, have a donkey farm in Kent. Ever since they came to have tea with us in the Spring and suggested that Nellie should bring us down to stay we've been begging Samuel to allow us to go. Samuel had eventually agreed, and as Flora had a half term holiday from her ballet school that October we were to leave the next morning.

So you see I was feeling pretty breezy at the prospect of five whole days without any Latin grammar lessons from Mr Willoughby, and although Flora wouldn't admit it for the world I could tell that she was quite looking forward to a break from her ballet lessons. Flora takes her ballet very seriously. She's decided that she's going to be a dancer, and she's always going on about Madame Zhinovia, her new teacher, and the dedication you need if you're going to become a world famous ballerina. In fact, she'd been lecturing me about that very subject as we walked back from the tram stop together, until I started ribbing her a bit, the way I do when I can see that she's getting too pompous. Flora is eleven, two years younger than I am, and she doesn't much like being teased. Anyway, I'd grabbed her shoe bag and held it up over my head for a while as we walked along, to test her jetée's, and she'd gone quite pink in the face with the effort of trying to reach it and had begun flailing about with her fists in a very unladylike way. Then I told her that I'd race her home because a great dancer needs plenty of running practice. Of course that made her more furious than ever and by the time we reached the front door we were both out of breath and Flora's face had turned from pink to scarlet.

I got inside the front door just before she did, and there was the letter. Flora must have realised at once that something pretty important had happened because of the way I dropped the shoe bag on the floor. I shook her off and picked up the letter.

"What is it?" She asked.

"Look," I said. "It's come by special delivery – that means it must be very urgent." Flora twitched the letter out of my hand and stared at it.

"What funny writing," she said, wrinkling up her nose. "All spiky and tailly. Who do you suppose it can be from, William?"

We were so absorbed in staring at the letter that we didn't hear Nellie coming up the stairs from the kitchen.

"Caught yer both at it, 'aven't I?" She said, appearing round the corner out of nowhere, or so it seemed, and stabbing a hair pin back into her bun. "Yer come up them steps just now like a herd of wild elephants and then silence, so I know'd just wot yer'd be doin' – and 'ere you are," she added, looking from one to the other of us with a glint in her eye. Flora was still holding the letter.

"Don't be cross, Nellie," she said, wriggling a little. "You must admit it's rather mysterious. Look, it says 'Special Delivery . . .'"

"I can read, same as you," Nellie snapped.

"Anyway, we were only looking," I said. "Do you know who it's from?"

"No, Mr Nosey Parker, I do not," Nellie said. "And wot's more it ain't none of my business – nor yours, nor Flora's. That letter is addressed to Samuel Rolandson, and when 'e gets 'ome I shouldn't wonder if 'e won't want to open it and read it for himself. So meantime perhaps you'd like ter leave it where I put it – on that there hall chair – that is if yer wants any cherry cake," she finished triumphantly.

"Cherry cake?" Flora said, suddenly losing interest in the letter and dropping it back on the hall chair as though it was nothing more unusual than the monthly bill from the butcher. "With icing?" I wouldn't say that Flora is greedy exactly, but she does enjoy her food.

"'Alf term, ain't it?" Nellie said, extricating herself from the hug that Flora was giving her and doing her best to look severe, even though I could tell that underneath she was pleased. "Now off yer go and wash yer 'ands and face for tea, Miss Muck. You too, William. Yer look like a couple of workhouse ragamuffins and no mistake. Wot you been doin' on the way 'ome, I'd like ter know?"

"Nothing special," Flora said airily.

"I suppose that's wot took yer so long," Nellie sniffed. But

Flora's mind was on the cherry cake, and before Nellie could remind her about hanging up her shoe bag in the right place she had swooped it up from the floor and vanished down the stairs. We heard her take the last four in one. "Don't you touch that icing, mind," Nellie called after her.

Left alone in the hall I went over and inspected the letter once more. The tall, spiky handwriting seemed more mysterious than ever, and I frowned as I nudged the letter straight on the chair, trying to imagine who on earth it could be from, and wishing that Samuel would hurry up and come home, so that he could open it and explain. Of course unusual and exciting events do happen quite often in our family, and I suppose that's only to be expected. You see, Samuel Rolandson, who is our Guardian, is a magician.

Samuel didn't arrive home until six o'clock, and before I tell you what happened when he did get back, and how the letter itself was only the first of the many strange events which followed, I had better explain a little more about Flora and Nellie and me, and about Samuel himself. I'll begin with Samuel, because if he hadn't found first me, and then Flora and adopted us, we shouldn't be a family at all, and Flora and I would probably have been brought up in some workhouse orphanage. We'd have had short hair and shapeless clothes to wear, I daresay, just like the orphanage children we often saw through the gates of the workhouse at the end of Kennington Road. I shouldn't have been learning Latin from Mr Willoughby and Flora wouldn't be taking ballet lessons from Madame Zhinovia, and there would be no visits to see Samuel backstage at the theatre, and no Nellie, and no half term teas with iced cherry cake.

The way in which Samuel came to find me was almost as strange as the way in which he came to find Flora. He wasn't a stage magician in those days; it was only later that he became the Astonishing Rolandson. At that time he was in South Africa where he had just discovered and then lost the most enormous diamond.

But that's part of another story. He had been away from England for a long time, first in India as a soldier, and then in South Africa, and I suppose that losing the diamond must have been an awful blow to him. That was why he decided to return home to England. The journey to the coast was very dangerous because there was a war going on at the time, so Samuel travelled with a party of English and Dutch settlers. But half way to the coast their party was attacked by the native Zulus, and when morning came the only survivors were Samuel and a baby who had remained hidden under one of the covered wagons during the fighting. That baby was me. Samuel made a sling, strapped me to his back and, collecting together all the water he could find, set off on horseback. He never expected to arrive at the coast, but by some miracle he did, and somehow I had survived as well. My mother and father had both been killed by the Zulus, and although Samuel tried to find out whether I had any other relations, no one seemed to know. So in the end he brought me to England and adopted me legally. It was then that he went into the Music Hall and became a stage magician, and not long afterwards, when he was just beginning to make a name for himself as the Astonishing Roland-son, Flora and Nellie both arrived on the scene.

Flora's entrance was quite dramatic, and she never gets tired of hearing Nellie tell the story of how it happened. Samuel was appearing at the Holborn Empire Theatre at the time, and Nellie was working there too as a stage dresser to Miss Vesta Tilley. She happened to be standing in the wings, watching Samuel's act, and she was as surprised as everyone else when she saw Samuel open a box which should have contained a white rabbit, and pull out a baby instead. Now none of us truly knows to this day how that baby, who was Flora of course, came to be in the box, not even Samuel who was utterly amazed himself. But with great presence of mind he lifted Flora out and showed her to the audience who thought it was part of the act and applauded and cheered till they nearly brought the house down. Samuel couldn't very well put Flora back in the box, though, so he strode off into the wings, and seeing Nellie standing there with her mouth open, he shoved the infant Flora into her arms. And that, as Nellie always says, is how she came to be left holding the baby. No one ever claimed Flora, and as time went on, I suppose that Samuel decided to make a proper job of it, since he'd already adopted me. So he adopted Flora as well, and Nellie, who couldn't bear to be parted from the baby, moved in to look after us. Flora has always been the apple of her eye.

So as you can see, Flora and I are not properly brother and sister, Samuel isn't our father but our Guardian, and Nellie is the closest we shall ever get to having a real mother. But I suppose that being such an unusual family has drawn us all closer together, and if you're beginning to feel sorry for Flora and me, being motherless orphans, I can tell you that you needn't, because there isn't a family in the land that either of us would want to change places with.

By the time that tea was over and Flora and I had done full justice to the iced cherry cake, the hands of the kitchen clock had moved round to twenty to six, but there was still no sign of Samuel. Nellie had been telling us Flora's second favourite story, which she always keeps for special occasions and is about the famous actress, Ellen Terry, and how her wig nearly caught fire when she was playing Lady Macbeth. She'd even put in the bit about the bracelet made of snakes, which she doesn't always do as it used to give us bad dreams when we were younger; and then, because we'd both begged her to tell us just once more, she'd gone on to the story of how Rose and Arthur had been able to buy The Cot and start their donkey farm all because Arthur had backed an outsider in the Derby and the horse had won.

I suppose that the effort of so much story telling must have exhausted Nellie, because after pouring the last squeezings from the tea pot into her cup, she had pushed aside the clothes horse which was all covered with neatly ironed and folded clothes ready for packing, and had sat down in the old rose patterned armchair beside the kitchen range, put her feet up on the fender and gone to sleep. All at once the kitchen was very quiet, so quiet that I could hear the ticking of the clock and the hiss of the gas lamps above the mantelshelf. Even Flora was unusually silent. It was as though we both knew that this was the calm before a great storm.

The distant rumble of a hansom made me look up at the clock again, but the hands didn't seem to have moved, and as the clip clop of hooves faded away into the distance I began to feel that I would burst if Samuel didn't come home soon and tell us who the letter was from. Flora must have felt the same, because she suddenly gave a little shiver and looked across at me.

"I wish that Samuel would come back," she whispered. "I feel as though I'm waiting for something, but I don't know what it is."

"It's the letter," I said very softly. Nellie's eyes had been closed, but now they opened with a snap.

"What are you two whispering about?" She asked.

"We weren't," Flora said. "Were we, William? Just talking softly so as not to wake you up."

"Fiddle de dee," Nellie sniffed. "I've told yer before, I can't abide whispering."

"Well let's do something then," I said, jumping up. "What about playing cards?"

"Cards!" Nellie exclaimed, suddenly sitting bolt upright in the armchair. "With the packing not finished and I don't know what else ter be done . . ."

"Just until Samuel gets home," Flora said. "Then we'll both help you with the packing, won't we, William?"

"Racing Demon," I said, half way to the door. "We haven't played that for ages."

"Oh yes," Flora exclaimed, clapping her hands together, and

before Nellie could protest about how it makes the corners of the cards dog eared, I was through the door and making for the stairs.

Racing Demon is easily our favourite card game, because it's fast and furious and very exhilarating. Of course you need one pack of cards each to play it, but one big advantage of having a stage magician for a Guardian is that there are always plenty of playing cards in the house. You see, Samuel uses a new pack for every performance.

The gas lamp on the landing was turned down low and the stairs were in shadow as I raced past the front door and towards the second flight that led to the bedrooms. It was then that I heard the sound of a hansom cab coming down the street, and thinking that it might be Samuel coming home at last I stopped and waited to see whether it would go past or stop. A moment later it drew up. I heard the cab man's voice, the jingle of coins, and then the sound of footsteps coming towards the front door.

"He's here," I shouted over the bannisters. "Samuel's here!"

But when I opened the front door the figure who stood silhouetted in the lamplight wasn't Samuel. For a moment I was too astonished to say a word, and I just stood there, staring at the tall, strange figure on the step. Then Flora was beside me.

"Jumping firecrackers. . . .!" She exclaimed. A flicker of a smile appeared on the stranger's impassive face, or so I thought. And then he bowed. He was distinctly Chinese. There could be no doubt about that. He wore a robe of some dark silk with huge sleeves into which his hands were tucked, and a Chinese hat that was like a large pill box. He looked exactly like the picture of a Chinese man that I'd seen in my Geography text book of Peoples of the World, and when he bowed I could see that he had a pigtail as well.

"Honourable Rolandson is at home, I think?" He said.

By this time Nellie must have realised that whoever was at the door it wasn't Samuel, because we could hear her beginning the ascent from the kitchen, and coming closer every moment. The Chinese gentleman bowed again and Flora and I stared at one another.

"Honourable Rolandson lives here?" he asked.

"Er – yes. Yes, he does," I mumbled.

"But he's not at home yet," Flora said. "Who are you?" But the Chinese gentleman didn't have a chance to reply, because at that moment Nellie arrived.

Nellie's years as a theatrical dresser have left their mark on her and she's used to queer customers who arrive unexpectedly backstage and knock at the doors she's in charge of. She stiffened a bit, and her face grew sharp with suspicion as she advanced and peered up into the stranger's face, thrusting both Flora and me to one side.

"'Oo are yer, and wot's yer business?" she asked sharply. "If you're trying to sell anything then yer've come to the wrong house. We don't need no brushes or ribbons, nor lamps neither, come to that," she added, looking the stranger up and down as though he had stepped out of the pantomime of Aladdin and had come to exchange new lamps for old. After a moment he bowed again.

"I am old friend of Honourable Rolandson," he said. "From China. Honourable Rolandson expects me, I think."

"He most certainly does not," Nellie said, taking a firmer grip on the door and beginning to edge it shut.

"I wrote letter to Honourable Rolandson," he said quickly. "It did not arrive?"

"I don't know nothin' about no letter," Nellie said. "Yer'll 'ave ter come back later, when Mr Rolandson is 'ere."

"Hang on a minute, Nellie," I cut in. "That letter for Samuel . . . the one that came today . . . it must be from him."

"Special delivery," the Chinese gentleman nodded. Nellie hesitated for a moment, rubbing at the rheumatism in her back and peering doubtfully round at the letter which still lay on the hall chair.

"Here," I said, picking it up and showing it to him. "Is this from you?"

"That is most certainly the letter," he said. "And now you say that Honourable Rolandson is not at home?"

"Oh we're expecting him back," Flora cut in. "We thought it was him coming up the steps – that's why William opened the door. Only it turned out to be you."

"Ah so," I thought I saw an expression of relief on his face, and he turned to Nellie again. "In that case, Honourable lady, you permit that I come into your house and wait?"

"Now 'ang on a minute," Nellie said sharply, "I don't permit no such thing."

But it was too late, for already the Chinese gentleman had stepped neatly inside and was standing in our front hall.

"Business most urgent," he said, giving a polite bow. "Many apologies for inconvenience. No need for alarm."

"Of all the cheek," Nellie exclaimed, looking thoroughly flustered by now. "'Ow dare yer – "

"Honourable Rolandson will be pleased that you have welcomed old friend," the Chinese gentleman murmured as though he would like to soothe Nellie's fears. "You have perhaps a fire? Night air in London is cold after long journey." Nellie stabbed ferociously at a hair pin and then jerked her head in the direction of the drawing room door, which stood ajar.

"You'd best wait in 'ere," she told him, "since you're in the 'ouse now. But I warn you that if Samuel Rolandson comes 'ome, which 'e will do shortly, and you ain't wot yer say . . ."

"Old friend," the Chinese gentleman murmured again. "No need for alarm," and after bowing once more he glided past us and went into the drawing room.

"Old friend, my foot," Nellie muttered darkly. "This is all your doing, William. You never ought to 'ave shown 'im the letter."

"It's too late now," I said, looking past her towards the drawing room. Through the open door I could see the stranger standing with his back to the fire, his hands still tucked deep into his sleeves. "Anyway, Samuel will be home soon."

"I just 'ope you're right," Nellie said in a low voice. "I don't like the looks of 'im and that's a fact. So you two stay out 'ere, and if you 'ear me give a shout then yer can both run for the police. I'm goin' in ter keep an eye on 'im . . . banging into other folks' houses uninvited – the very idea of it." And seizing Samuel's old thorn walking stick from the umbrella stand with a flourish, she followed the stranger into the drawing room and shut the door behind her.

"Perhaps he is a burglar," Flora said, taking hold of my arm. "Did you see what he did when he went in there . . ."

"Ssh," I told her. "I'm trying to listen." Through the door I could hear Nellie's voice rising and falling, and then the low murmur of the Chinese gentleman's reply, but I couldn't make out the words.

"What's happening?" Flora asked after a moment. "Here, let me have a look through the keyhole."

It was just then that we heard the sound of someone whistling Pop goes the Weasel, and footsteps hurrying up the front steps.

"Samuel!" Flora cried, as the key turned in the lock and the door swung open.

"There you both are," Samuel said, seeing us standing there. "I know I'm a little late, but I have some very exciting news to tell you all. Where's Nellie?" He twirled his hat on to the top of the hat stand and uncoiled his white silk scarf.

"In there," I said, pointing towards the drawing room. "And it's just as well you're back – "

"Because we've got something to tell you, too," Flora nodded. But Samuel wasn't listening. He was smiling in a way I'd never seen him smile before.

"Chang is coming to London," he said. "The Great Chang. Probably the greatest magician in the world, and a very old friend of mine. I've known for some time, but I didn't want to tell you before now because – " He broke off for a moment and looked at us with his head on one side. "What on earth is the matter with you both?" He asked. "You look as if you've seen a ghost. And you've both got your mouths wide open."

"He's here," I said.

"Here?" Samuel said. "Surely not. . . . Where?"

"In the drawing room," Flora cut in. "With Nellie – "

"He wrote to you," I said. "Only the letter didn't arrive until this afternoon. Here it is."

"And Nellie's got your walking stick," Flora said. "She thinks he's a burglar."

"Does she indeed?" Samuel said, putting his hand on the door knob. "Then I think I'd better see for myself what's going on."

I suppose that when two magicians meet after many years you would expect something strange and exciting to happen, such as a burst of Catherine wheels, or a thunderclap, or at the very least a cloud of brilliant silk scarves to come floating down from the heavens. But I can't tell you exactly what did happen at the moment when the Great Chang and the Astonishing Rolandson met, because Samuel was already inside the drawing room and he had closed the door behind him.

CHAPTER TWO

In which we are shut out, and the moonlight reveals a strange sight . . .

Flora and I stared at one another in shocked silence. It wasn't like Samuel to shut us out. But he had done so this time. There had been no mistaking the unexpected firmness with which he'd closed the door behind him.

"Why aren't we allowed to go in?" Flora said in a low voice.

"I don't know," I muttered. I would have liked to give the door a good thump with my foot. It seemed very unfair, specially when it was me who had guessed the letter was from Chang. If Nellie had had her way he would have been half way across Lambeth Bridge in a hansom cab by then, instead of warming himself beside our fire. And now Nellie was in the drawing room with him, and we were outside in the hall. Flora was still gazing at the door as though she expected it to fly open at any moment.

"Samuel never shuts us out," she said, shaking her head in a baffled way. "Never . . . does he? Don't you think it's odd, William?"

I had given up trying to make out what Samuel and Chang were saying. The drawing room door was too thick and I guessed that they were at the far end of the room beside the fire. All I could hear was a sort of low mumbling. When I didn't answer Flora came and sat beside me on the stairs.

"If you ask me," she went on, "the whole thing is odd. Chang turning up unexpectedly like this, and Samuel not telling us he was coming to London until he'd actually arrived." She frowned. "You'd think he would have wanted us to know if they're such old friends. And there's another thing . . ." She moved closer to me. "Did you notice what Chang did when he went into the drawing room? I tried to tell you before, only you shushed me." Her voice sank to a whisper. "He closed the curtains . . ."

"I don't see what's odd about that," I told her. But Flora shook her head.

"You don't understand. It was the way he did it – sort of quickly, and standing to one side. As though he didn't want to be seen from outside."

"I think you're imagining it," I said after a moment, doing my best to sound matter of fact. "You're always imagining things."

"No I'm not," Flora said. "This wasn't one of my hunches if that's what you're thinking. I just happened to notice it, that's all. And now I'm more certain than ever that something peculiar is happening, otherwise why would Samuel have shut us out?" We both looked at the drawing room door. It was gloomy in the hall, and a gust of wind beating suddenly against the front door made the flame in the gas lamp jump and splutter. In spite of myself I felt a shiver go down my spine.

And then, from inside the room we heard Samuel starting to laugh.

"This is too tantalising for words," Flora exclaimed, jumping up. "If I don't find out what's going on I shall burst. I'm going to look through the keyhole."

She was just getting down on to her hands and knees when the door flew open, and Nellie came out with such suddenness that she nearly sent Flora flying. She was carrying the coal scuttle and looking rather agitated.

"Listening at keyholes, wos yer?" She snapped, closing the door quickly behind her as Flora stumbled to her feet. "Just wot I thought. Well it's downstairs into the kitchen wiv the pair of yer, and look sharp about it." And taking a firm hold of Flora's arm and thrusting the coal scuttle into my hands she propelled us both towards the stairs before we could protest.

"What's happening, Nellie?" Flora burst out as soon as we were in the kitchen. "Why did Samuel shut us outside? And why can't we go and meet Chang properly? What's all the mystery?"

"There ain't no mystery as I'm aware of," Nellie retorted.

"Then why wouldn't Samuel let us come in?" I asked.

"Unheard of, ain't it?" Nellie said, lifting the kettle on to the range. "Something goin' on in this 'ouse and neither of yer bein' in on the act." She sniffed. "Yer pore little 'earts must be breakin'."

"If there's no mystery then there's nothing wrong in wanting to know," I frowned. "Is there?"

"And nothing wrong in Samuel wanting to 'ave one of 'is oldest friends wot 'e 'asn't seen for years and years to 'imself for five minutes either," Nellie said, stabbing a hair pin back into her bun.

"I suppose not," Flora said doubtfully.

"So there's no call ter go making a great mystery out of it just because yer was included out for once."

"I wish you'd tell us all the same," I said. "I mean – the greatest magician in the world comes to our house and first we're shut out in the hall and then we're banished to the kitchen."

"You must admit it's very aggravating," Flora nodded. "So please, Nellie dear, do tell us. . . . what happened?"

"You are a pair of pests and no mistake," Nellie declared. But I saw that she had screwed her face into quite a loving expression all the same.

"Tell us," I insisted.

"Well, if yer really wants ter know," she began, and then stopped.

"Go on," Flora begged, taking both Nellie's hands. "Please . . ."

"I suppose they shook hands," I said.

"More of a hug I'd call it," Nellie said. "Don't seem as though them Chinese go in much for 'and shaking." She sniffed. "'E didn't shake 'ands wiv me neither. Just bowed – all stately like when Samuel introduced us." She gave a twitch to her apron and straightened her back.

"And then?" I said.

"And that was that," Nellie answered. For a moment there was silence.

"Nothing else?" Flora asked. "Nothing?"

"Wot did yer expect? A puff of smoke, I suppose . . . or a thunder flash."

"There must have been more to it than that," I said. "You were in there for ages." Nellie put her head on one side.

"Ooh yer, now I come ter think of it there was one other thing," she said, with a little nod.

"What?" We both asked.

"Samuel told me they'd like some tea," Nellie said, "that's wot. And if you two would stop chattering at me I'd be able ter get on and make it. Fetch them cups from the dresser, will yer, Flora? And you, William, go and fill the coal scuttle, there's a good boy."

Flora and I looked at one another. Nellie can be as close as an oyster when she puts her mind to it, and I could see by the expression on her face that it would be useless to go on wheedling. So I picked up the coal scuttle and went towards the back door.

The tray was all ready when I came back into the kitchen. Nellie had put out the best china, and the silver tea pot which is generally kept for very special occasions, such as Christmas, or when Samuel's sister, Gus comes to stay, so I knew she was doing her best to make a good impression. She'd even sliced up the last of the cherry cake into neat, finger shaped pieces and arranged them on our finest cake plate.

"Right, that's the lot," she said, casting a final look over the tray and giving her apron another twitch. "Open that door for me, William."

"Why don't you let me take the tray," Flora said quickly, giving Nellie her best smile and fluttering her eyelashes. "It looks awfully heavy. And William could bring the coal scuttle." But Nellie was unmoved.

"Oh no yer don't, Miss Muck," she said, grasping the handles of the tea tray and giving Flora quite a sharp look. 'Yer don't get round me like that. I know you're both dyin' ter get in on the act, but this time, yer can't."

"Do you mean we're not going to be allowed to see Chang at all?" Flora asked, her face falling. "Not even for a minute?"

"That's not for me to say," Nellie told her, picking up the tray. "All I know is that they wants their tea in peace and quiet. Samuel's orders." she added ominously. Flora and I looked at one another. Samuel very seldom gives orders, and on the rare occasions when he does, he means you to obey them.

"But why?" I frowned. Nellie tightened her lips.

"If you ask me that Mr Chang is quite wore out with all the travelling 'e's done, and 'e don't want ter be gawped at by a couple of kids. So don't you go following me upstairs again."

"Gawped at indeed," Flora exclaimed, as soon as Nellie had gone. "I never gawp."

"You stare, though, don't you," I grinned at her. Flora opened her mouth, but I went on quickly. "Look," I said, "it's no use. You heard what Nellie said. If it's Samuel's orders that's that." After a moment she nodded. Then she wetted her fingers and ran it round the plate where the cherry cake had been, gathering up the last of the crumbs.

"There's more to this than Nellie's letting on," she said thoughtfully. "I'm sure of it. There is a mystery . . ."

I suppose that if we had been an ordinary family, with an ordinary mother and father to look after us, Flora and I wouldn't have minded nearly so much being shut out of the drawing room and not being allowed to meet such an important guest. If we had been an ordinary family our mother would have been forever reminding us that children should be seen and not heard, and that grown ups know best and we shouldn't ask so many questions. But as I remarked before we're not an ordinary family. Luckily for us no one has ever told us that children should be seen and not heard, and Samuel has never minded how many questions we ask. He isn't in the least like most grown ups who always seem to be rushing about and only giving you half their attention. He listens to us and answers our questions in a proper way, and if something is worrying us he always seems to know. What's more he tells us his plans and quite often asks us what we think.

And that was another thing. Why hadn't Samuel told us that Chang was coming to London? The more I thought about it the more puzzling it all became, and the worst part of all was that the next day we were leaving for the country. If we didn't see Chang that evening we might never see him again.

Flora and I were leaning on the kitchen table and building a castle with the sugar knobs when Nellie came back into the room. I could see at once that she had something to tell us.

"It seems like yer wishes 'as been granted after all," she announced, looking from one to the other of us and not appearing to notice the sugar knobs. "Yer going' ter be allowed upstairs to the drawing room."

We both made a dive for the door. Flora, being nearer to it, got there first.

"But not yet," Nellie went on, closing it smartly and holding one hand up in the air as though she was a policeman. "Yer can go in a quarter of an hour, Samuel says, and that's just long enough for yer both ter give me a 'and with these tea things and get tidied up."

At the mention of getting tidied up Flora immediately began

smoothing her hair and twitching at her skirt, and then studying her feet, so that I knew what was coming.

"Shall I go and put on my new merino?" She asked. I'm afraid to say that Flora is rather vain and there's nothing she likes better than dressing up. Most people think her very pretty, especially when she flutters her eyelashes and smiles, and Nellie's always going on about the colour of her hair, which she says is like ripe hazelnuts, and her lovely dark eyelashes, and all this just encourages Flora, so that she's for ever wanting to put on her best clothes and pose in front of the looking glass. But this time Nellie shook her head.

"No time for all that today," she said firmly. "You two seem to 'ave forgotten that we're goin' away tomorrow morning, and there's a load of things to do before then. A lick and a promise will 'ave ter do for the Great Chang. And you, William, clear up them sugar knobs. If I've told yer once I've told yer a thousand times – I can't abide yer breathing over the sugar."

"Yes, Nellie," I said meekly. It was no time to argue.

Fifteen minutes later exactly Flora and I were standing upstairs in the front hall. Nellie had knocked so discreetly on the drawing room door and was wearing such a respectful expression that for a moment I felt as though we were visitors in someone else's house, instead of being at home in our own.

"Yer not ter stay long, mind," she whispered to us as she turned the handle. "I wants yer both upstairs in ten minutes to 'elp me wiv the packing." Then, pushing the door open, she nodded to us to go in.

The drawing room is Nellie's pride and joy, but of all the rooms in our house it's the one I like least of all. It's a big room, full of stiff, unfriendly furniture, such as armchairs draped with antimacassars and little tables on spindly legs which fall over if you so much as look at them and send ornaments and silver photograph frames flying. Once a week Nellie polishes all the furniture and dusts the ornaments on the mantelpiece and all the little tables and beats the rugs, and every day from October to May when Samuel isn't at the theatre she lights the fire at half past three in case he wants to go in there to read, or write letters. But she always closes the door behind her. It's that kind of room, which is why Flora and I don't go in there very often, and whenever we do we're both horribly aware of having to be on our best behaviour.

After the cheerful brightness of the kitchen, the drawing room seemed even more unfamiliar and gloomy than usual that evening. The oil lamp on the table was turned down to a dim glow, and the only other light came from the flames of the fire which threw flickering shadows on the walls and gave the furniture a mysterious, lumpy look, as though a lot of strange animals were arranged about the room in odd places. Samuel was standing beside the fire at the far end of the room, speaking to Chang in a low voice, but he looked up when we came in and held out his hand to us.

"There you both are," he said. "Come over here and say your how-do-you do's. I know you've already met, unofficially, but now I want to introduce you both properly to the Great Chang – probably the greatest magician in the world, and the man who taught me everything I know." He put his arm round my shoulder, and taking Flora's hand he drew us both over towards the wing chair where Chang was sitting. "Chang, my dear fellow, allow me to introduce my wards to you, William and Flora."

In the shadowy gloom it was hard to make out the expression on the Great Chang's face, and he sat so still in the depths of the armchair that for a moment before he leant forward I had the odd sensation that he wasn't really a living, breathing human being at all. Then I heard the silk of his robe rustle.

"Chang much honoured to meet you," he murmured. "William. And Flora."

It would have been the moment to shake hands, except that Chang's were still tucked into the sleeves of his robe, and after

Flora and I had mumbled 'How do you do', there was an awkward silence and I saw Flora glance helplessly at Samuel.

"Well, that's that then," Samuel smiled. "Introductions over."

"Not quite," Chang murmured. "Chang wishes to thank Honourable children."

"Thank us," Flora frowned. "Whatever for?" A hint of a smile appeared on his face, and then he leant back again in the shadows of the chair.

"Quickness of thought saved Chang from fate worse than death."

"Double pneumonia at the very least, I should say," Samuel nodded.

"Oh, you mean the letter," Flora said. "Well, that was William really, not me. Though I suppose I would have guessed in the end." She looked at me, and then went on confidentially. "Nellie didn't mean to be rude, you know. It was a bit of a shock, that's all."

"To see strange Oriental gentleman in respectable neighbourhood?" Chang asked gently, but somehow I felt he was laughing at her.

"Dear old Nellie," Samuel said, putting his hand on my shoulder as he spoke. "She can be quite a tiger when it comes to defending hearth and home. Her face was a study, I can tell you, when she saw Chang and me embracing like the long lost friends we are. But it was lucky you had your wits about you, otherwise I don't suppose Chang would have got past the front door, and that might have turned out to be quite a calamity." I frowned, not knowing quite what to say. Even with Samuel's hand on my shoulder and hearing the natural, easy way he spoke, I still felt that something about the conversation was odd and out of place, though I couldn't work out then what it was. There was silence for a moment or two until Flora, who had been staring very fixedly at Chang, suddenly said: "Is it really true that you were Samuel's teacher?"

"Perfectly true," Samuel said. "And a magnificent teacher he was, too."

"You were most apt and intelligent pupil I think," Chang said. "The good pupil makes the good master."

"Well that means you could tell us how all Samuel's tricks are done," Flora went on. "He won't ever tell us anything at all, will he, William? No matter how often we ask."

"Would you tell us?" I asked, looking directly at the Great Chang. He returned my gaze for a moment, and then looked up at Samuel.

"Some secrets are made to be kept," he murmured, inclining his head slightly. "Some tales are long in telling."

"Now you're talking in riddles," Flora frowned. "Whatever does that mean?"

"It means," said Samuel with a laugh, "that Chang won't give away trade secrets any more than I will, and in any case that's quite enough questions for the moment. I can't allow you to catechise him as you do me. He's had a long journey. Besides," he went on, "now that Chang has come to London at last he intends to be here for some time, I'm glad to say, and later on, after all this is over – "

"All what?" I cut in. Samuel paused for a moment and glanced at Chang, and as he did so one of the lumps of coal in the grate suddenly spurted into flame so that I saw in the blaze the tiny line that had appeared between his eyebrows. There was a faint rustle as Chang straightened himself a little in the armchair; and then Samuel smiled.

"You see how hard it is to keep a secret in this house, my dear fellow," he said lightly. "Well? What do you say? Now that I've let the cat out of the bag, shall we tell them?"

"Yes, tell us, do. Please tell us," Flora begged. Another look passed between Samuel and Chang.

"There can be no harm in it," Samuel said after a moment. "I had meant to keep the news until you came back from The Cott, but you may as well know now." He paused, looking from one to the other of us. "Chang is to open at the Alhambra shortly in his own magic show," he said.

"The Alhambra," Flora cried, clapping her hands. "Oh, how wonderful. It's my favourite theatre. Can we go? We can, can't we, Samuel? Can we go to the first night?"

"I'm not making any promises about the first night," Samuel said. "But as soon as you get back from Kent we'll see about some tickets – and in the stage box. There now, are you both satisfied?"

Flora clapped her hands again, several times, and showed signs of doing a pirouette as well, until Samuel laid a restraining hand on her shoulder, after which she declared that going to the Alhambra to see Chang would be the most exciting night of her life. There wasn't much more to be said, because of course I had to agree that it would be very thrilling to watch the greatest magician the world had ever known.

All the same I had a nagging feeling at the back of my mind that Samuel hadn't said everything there was to say, and before I went to sleep that night I remembered about the line between his brows. I've seen that line before, and it generally means that he's worried about something, but doesn't want to say what it is.

But that was much later, after Samuel announced that our ten minutes was up and that it was time we said goodnight and went upstairs. By then all that Flora could think about was telling Nellie that we were going to have seats in the stage box at the Alhambra to see Chang, so that she quite forgot to say goodnight properly and after declaring once again that it would be the most exciting night of her life she ran to the door and raced upstairs two at a time, calling Nellie at the top of her voice. Samuel watched her go, and then put his hand on my shoulder and walked me to the door.

"Do your best to keep her quiet, will you, dear boy?" He murmured. "Chang is very tired after his journey, and we have a great deal to talk about."

"I'll do my best," I nodded. I hesitated, twiddling with the door knob. Samuel gave me one of his special smiles.

"When old friends meet after many years there's always a lot to talk about," he said, answering my unspoken question. "So don't feel too upset about being shut out this evening. Chang will still be here when you get back from Kent."

"Yes, of course," I said. "Well – good night."

"Good night, dear boy," Samuel said.

Just before he closed the door I looked back for an instant into the room. The fire had burnt low and although I could make out the shadowy outline of the wing chair, I couldn't see Chang at all. It was almost as though he wasn't really there. Then Samuel closed the door, and I went upstairs to find Flora and Nellie.

The packing was in full swing, and it wasn't until much later, when the last bag had been closed and Nellie had laid out the clothes we were to put on in the morning and sewn on several buttons and ironed the last two shirts and reminded us both for the hundredth time that we had an early start, that I was at last alone and able to think things over. I lay for a long time staring at the shadows which my candle made on the ceiling and listening to the low murmur of voices in the drawing room below where Samuel and Chang were still talking. We had been looking forward to going to The Cott for months, but now, suddenly, I wasn't sure that I wanted to go after all. There were so many questions I would have liked to ask Samuel, and I knew that I shouldn't be able to find out the answers for a whole week.

At last I must have fallen asleep, because when I opened my eyes again the candle had burnt itself out and the house was still and silent. Outside the moon shone, high in the sky. Chang must have left, I thought, and Samuel was probably asleep too. I wondered what time it was, and after turning my pillows several times and straightening the blankets which had come untucked, I decided to go and look. You can see the clock on Kennington Church tower from my bedroom window, and I guessed that the moonlight was bright enough for me to be able to make out the hands.

The street was deserted, so I knew that it must be very late, and as I stood there, waiting for the moon to come out from behind a small patch of cloud, I heard a sort of rumbling. The sound came closer, and the next moment I saw a figure wheeling a hand cart along the street. When he was opposite our house, he stopped and looked up.

He must have stood there, quite still, for about a minute. Then the moon came out from behind the cloud and as it did so he moved quickly on. The rumbling grew fainter and disappeared, and in the silence that followed I pinched myself, just to make sure that I was awake. Because the figure I had seen in the street below was a Chinese man. And the strange thing was that I knew it wasn't Chang.

CHAPTER THREE

In which we visit the country, and events take an unexpected turn.

Nellie had said that she would wake us at crack of dawn and she was as good as her word. It was still pitch dark outside when I woke to hear the familiar thump of the hot water can on my bedroom floor and the sound of Nellie striking a match to light the lamp. After opening one eye I quickly closed it again as the gas light popped into life and buried my head under the bedclothes.

"You awake, William?" Nellie said. "Time ter get up."

"But it's still dark," I grumbled, burrowing further into the blankets. "It's the middle of the night."

"Six thirty," Nellie replied, "and there's a lot to do if we're goin' ter catch that train at ten o'clock."

"What train?" I muttered, opening both eyes this time.

"Lor bless the boy – yer surely ain't forgotten where we're goin', 'ave yer?" Nellie asked, pouring the hot water into the bowl.

"Oh – that train," I said stupidly, suddenly remembering about The Cott as well as everything else that had happened the night before.

"Arthur'll be there to meet us at the station," Nellie went on. "He'll be bringing the donkey cart I shouldn't wonder – now up yer get while this water's still nice and hot. Flora's almost dressed and breakfast will be ready soon." And before I had a chance to ask her whether Samuel was going to come down to see us off she had gone.

I rolled over and sat up, rubbing the sleep out of my eyes, and the first thing I saw were my best clothes sitting on the chair where Nellie had laid them out the night before. So I lay down again and pulled the covers back over me, just for a minute or two, and thought how much more fun journeys would be if you could wear your oldest clothes.

Of course, travelling always seems to bring out the worst in Nellie. She plans every journey as though she's going to deepest Africa and won't be back for a year, if at all. This means being prepared, and always packing six vests when two would do, just in case, and not forgetting all sorts of things that you could easily do without in my opinion, such as needles and thread and cakes of soap and sticking plasters and boot polish and spare boot laces. All this makes the luggage rather heavy, and we generally end up having to take an extra bag so that Nellie can stuff into it all the things she's suddenly remembered at the last minute when all the other bags have been locked and corded down. Worst of all, since going anywhere means travelling on a train and in a hansom cab and being seen in public, Nellie always insists that we wear our most respectable clothes, with gloves to keep our hands clean and hats to keep our hair tidy, which quite spoils the thrill of the whole thing.

All this was flashing through my mind as I lay there, trying to pluck up the nerve to put my feet on to the cold oil cloth and begin struggling into the stiff, starched shirt that Nellie had laid out for me, when Flora burst into the room. She was fully dressed and was carrying her hair brush.

"Guess what?" she said.

"You might knock," I told her crossly.

"Well you should be up by now," she countered. "Why aren't you? Nellie brought your water ages ago. It must be cold." Flora's horribly brisk in the mornings. "Quite cold," she said, going over and swishing it about with her finger. "Ice cold in fact. Listen, William, I came to tell you . . . Chang's still here. He spent the night in the spare back bedroom."

"How do you know?" I asked, sitting bolt upright and staring at her.

"Nellie let it out by mistake," Flora said, perching on the end of the bed. "To tell you the truth I don't think she was meant to tell, but when we were getting dressed she was muttering about being up till all hours making beds, and when I said did she mean Chang had spent the night here, in our house, she gave me one of her looks and wouldn't say another word. Anyway, I went along there. I was just going to take a peep to see what he looked like asleep and what he did with his pigtail – "

"You mean you actually went into his room?"

"Well – no. I couldn't. That's what I'm trying to tell you. The door was locked, you see. Don't you think that's odd?"

"No, I don't," I said. "I expect Samuel warned him. And it was a good thing he did. You're always bouncing into people's rooms, and he knew that's just what you'd do if you found out."

"William!" Flora said, looking quite shocked.

"Well you did, didn't you," I said.

"Ye-es," she agreed, wriggling a little. "I suppose I did. But only because of the pigtail. And now I'll probably never know."

"You could ask Samuel," I said. Then I frowned, suddenly remembering the figure I had seen through the window. "Flora – " I began. But she wasn't listening.

"Anyway, I've got to go downstairs," she said, jumping up and going towards the door. "Nellie's waiting to do my hair. And for goodness sake, William, get up – or we'll miss the train and it'll be all your fault."

"All right, all right," I muttered. "The train doesn't go for hours – not till ten o'clock."

"Don't you want to go to The Cott?" Flora asked, stopping by the door and giving me a very direct look.

"Of course I do," I said. "I like Arthur. He can juggle with three oranges. And he might take me to the dockyards at Chatham, Nellie said."

"There are the donkeys, too," Flora said. "And there isn't any mystery any more, is there? Not now we know Chang is opening at the Alhambra. I suppose that's what he and Samuel were talking about."

"I suppose so," I nodded. Flora twirled her hairbrush and looked at me again.

"I'll tell Nellie you're just coming," she said, and went out leaving the door wide open.

It wasn't that I didn't want to go to The Cott exactly. We had been looking forward to it ever since Arthur had come to our house in the summer and suggested to Nellie over tea in the kitchen that she should bring us down to spend a few days with him and Rose. We'd been counting off the days on the kitchen calendar. But after the Great Chang's unexpected arrival on our doorstep I had the strangest feeling that something was going to happen, and I would really rather have stayed at home to find out what it was. Flora had said that the mystery was over, but then she didn't know about the figure I had seen during the night, and on reflection I decided that it was just as well that I hadn't told her. She would only have said that I'd been dreaming; and it wasn't until much later on that I remembered what Flora had said about Chang pulling the curtains in the drawing room.

The kitchen clock was just striking seven when I got downstairs, and for the next two hours there wasn't a moment to think. Although Nellie had finished most of the packing the night before there still seemed to be a hundred and one things to be done, such as writing notes to the butcher and baker telling them when to call again, and riddling out the kitchen range and filling the coal scuttle, as well as stuffing dozens of things into the overflow bag, just in case. But at last Nellie announced that it was time for me to run to the corner and find a hansom, and to look sharp about it as it was nearly a quarter to nine.

By the time I arrived back with the hansom the bags were all ready and standing in a neat row in the front hall, Flora had her hat and coat and gloves on and Nellie was in front of the looking glass jabbing hat pins into her second best bonnet to skewer it into place. At the last moment Samuel appeared on the stairs in his dressing gown to say goodbye. It was too late by then to ask him all the questions I had wanted to ask. There was only just time to hug him goodbye and for Nellie to remind him of the last minute things she'd forgotten to say until that moment.

"There's a cold pie on the pantry shelf, and a fresh loaf. And a piece of stilton cheese . . . now yer won't forget to lock the back door at night, will yer – "

"And draw the bolts," Samuel murmured.

"I feel dreadful goin' off without doin' yer breakfast," Nellie said, shaking her head so that her bonnet trembled and tilted to one side. "Are yer sure yer'll be all right, Samuel?"

"Nellie, old dear, you're only going to be away for five days."

"All the same it doesn't seem right," Nellie said, looking more doubtful than ever and eyeing the luggage as though she had half a mind to take the bags back upstairs and unpack them all again. "Not now . . ."

"And don't you worry about Chang either," Samuel said firmly. "I'll look after him. We'll live like kings, put our feet up on the fender and feast on oysters and champagne. Now off you go, all of you. That hansom won't wait for ever."

"Is Chang going to stay here all the time we're away?" Flora asked. But at that moment the cab driver, who had grown tired of waiting, jumped down from the box and came up the path towards us.

"Look, Guvnor, do you want this cab or not?" He asked. That settled it.

In the final flurry of saying goodbye and loading the luggage, Samuel put his arm round my shoulder and slipping his hand into his dressing gown pocket he produced two gold sovereigns.

"I know you're only going to be away for five days, but in my experience a gentleman should never travel without adequate funds," he said gravely, putting the money into my hand. "This should cover all contingencies, I think. And take care of them both, won't you?" He nodded towards the hansom where Flora and Nellie were already stowed amongst the luggage.

"Of course," I said. "There were all sorts of things I wanted to ask you. But it's too late now, isn't it?"

"I have a feeling those questions can be answered when you get back," Samuel smiled.

"I expect so," I nodded.

"Now off you go, or Nellie will be in a fever about missing the train."

Even though I have travelled on such illustrious trains as the Flying Dutchman to Cornwall and the London and North Eastern Express to Scarborough, I still couldn't help feeling the familiar prickle of excitement down my spine as we climbed out of the hansom cab at London Bridge Station and made our way to the platform to board the train to Kent. One day I mean to travel on the Orient Express from Paris to Constantinople, but even a short train journey is a special event for me, and by the time the porter had arranged the bags in the rack above our heads and the doors were being slammed up and down the train, and the station clock stood at one minute to ten, I had forgotten all about the Great Chang and was waiting for the guard to blow his whistle and for the journey to begin.

"William, come back in 'ere," Nellie said, as she always did. "It's dangerous, 'anging out of the window like that."

"But we're not even moving yet. It can't be dangerous," I said, determined not to miss the hissing of the engine as it got up steam, or the magical moment when the guard blew his whistle and we began to move.

"We'll start with a jerk and you'll bang yer 'ead," Nellie said.

"Besides, it's cold in here," Flora said. "I'm freezing."

I suppose I should have had to give in, only at that moment I saw the guard lift the whistle to his lips, and as the sound echoed up and down the platform I felt the first lurch of the engine and we began to move.

"There," I said, closing the window and grinning at them both. "We're off!"

"Thanks for telling us," Nellie said with a sniff. "I do declare I 'adn't noticed, 'ad you, Flora?" Flora began to giggle and I glared at her. "I suppose yer'll condescend ter sit down now, will yer?" Nellie went on, "instead of bobbin' about like a parched pea and treading on my feet."

"Certainly," I said in my most dignified manner. Unfortunately at that moment the train went over some points and swayed so violently that I lost my balance and landed unceremoniously on the seat beside Flora, knocking my elbow and squashing her hat in the process. By the time we'd sorted ourselves out the rows of terraced houses were already beginning to give way to green fields and distant glimpses of the tall masts of sailing barges on the Thames, and we were chugging towards Greenwich and Blackheath.

"I'm hungry," Flora announced as we pulled out of Blackheath Station. "It seems hours since breakfast."

"And hours till lunch, too," I nodded. We both looked at Nellie.

"Lucky I remembered to make a few cheese sandwiches then, ain't it," she said. "Fetch down that overflow bag, William."

"Apples, too," Flora exclaimed as Nellie unpacked the picnic and laid it on the seat beside her.

34

After we'd finished eating and had cleared up the crumbs and the apple cores and the grease proof paper Nellie settled down for a doze, and while her bonnet slid slowly sideways until it finally came to rest over one eye, Flora and I counted cows and churches and drew on the windows, which were getting satisfyingly steamed up by then. When the windows were all used up I pulled out my notebook and pencil and we played noughts and crosses, until the train stopped once again at a station and looking out of the window I announced that the next stop would be ours. Nellie woke up with a start and straightened her bonnet, jabbing hat pins and hair pins back into place, and Flora wiped all our drawings off the windows with her sleeve so that we could see out.

"Best get them bags down, William," Nellie said, peering out and giving a quick nod. "We'll be there in next to no time. Look . . . there's the windmill I told yer both about. Flora, put yer gloves and 'at on again for mercy's sake and straighten yer skirt. And William, come over 'ere and let me get that smut off yer face."

If there's one thing I can't bear it's having my face scrubbed at with Nellie's pocket handkerchief, especially as she always spits on it first, but I could tell from the way she had gone so pink and was screwing her face up that she was feeling excited about seeing Rose and Arthur and wanted us to make a good impression, so I put up with it as well as I could until I felt the train beginning to slow down.

"I think we've arrived," I muttered, twisting my face away and peering over my shoulder at Flora, who was standing by the window.

"Yes," she nodded, cramming her hat on. "Look! I can see the station. And there's Arthur."

The next moment the train had jolted to a halt, and we were jumping down on to the platform and standing in the pale, bright sunlight. We could see Arthur, wearing a red and white spotted neckerchief and a curly brown bowler hat.

"We're here," Flora cried, rather unnecessarily I thought, since we were the only people getting off the train. "Here!"

"Hello my lovely," Arthur said, giving Flora a smacking kiss which made her blush, and then putting out his hand to me. "Welcome to Kent. Nellie, me old darling, 'ow are yer?"

"Not so bad Arthur," Nellie said. "'Ow's yerself?"

"*I'm* all right," Arthur said.

Something about the way he said it made me stiffen, and I saw Nellie give him a sharp look.

"Wot's up, Arthur?" she asked. Arthur pushed back his bowler hat and scratched his head.

"It's Rose," he said. "She wasn't feeling quite the thing this morning. To tell you the truth, I left 'er in bed."

"In bed?" Nellie said, raising her voice above the noise of the train which had begun to pull slowly out of the station on the last leg of its journey to Rochester. Flora and I looked at one another.

"It come on 'er sudden-like last night," Arthur nodded. "Else I would 'ave written yer not to come. But it was too late for that."

"Well this don't sound too good," Nellie said, studying the worried expression on Arthur's face, her head on one side. Now that the train had gone the platform seemed very quiet. "If she's that poorly 'adn't you better fetch the doctor to 'er?"

"I've done that already," Arthur nodded. "Left a note at 'is 'ouse on the way to the station. I'm glad you're 'ere, Nellie old girl," he added, "and that's a fact." Nellie gave a little shake of her head and clicked her tongue.

"No use standin' 'ere though, is it? If the doctor's on 'is way we'd best go and see wot's 'appening. Pick up them bags you two and look sharp about it."

It seemed an unlucky beginning for our holiday, and as Flora and I followed Nellie and Arthur out of the station not even the sight of the little grey donkey between the shafts of the cart could cheer us up.

No one spoke much on the way to The Cott. I had been looking forward to sitting in the front of the box beside Arthur, and maybe even taking the reins for a while, but when Nellie told me to hop up in the back with Flora I didn't have the heart to argue. We couldn't see the donkey, or the road ahead, just the solid shape of Arthur's back and his curly brimmed bowler, and beside him Nellie, sitting bolt upright and holding on to her bonnet first with one hand and then with the other to stop it blowing away. After turning round once to ask if we were all right Arthur didn't speak except to urge the donkey to go faster. Even Flora was silent, and in spite of it being such a fine day, with the sun shining out of a pale blue sky and the trees and hedges the colour of home made toffee, I grew gloomier and gloomier.

We must have been travelling for about ten minutes when Arthur turned round again, and pointing with his whip towards a cottage on a low green hill ahead of us said: "There's The Cott. We shan't be long now."

A minute or two later we turned into a small lane with hedges on each side. Ahead of us was a white gate, and beyond that, at the top of the rise, the cottage. Arthur reined in the donkey.

"This hill's a mite stiff for Bessie with the four of us in the cart," he said, "and it'll save me getting off the box if you two wouldn't mind opening the gate and then following us on up to The Cott."

"Good idea, Arthur." Nellie nodded. "A bit of exercise won't do them no 'arm after being cooped up on that train."

"You can 'ave a look at the donkeys on the way," Arthur told us as we clambered down into the lane. "And don't forget to latch the gate after you. We don't want none of them getting out." He cracked his whip, and Bessie, sensing home and her own stable ahead of her, trotted eagerly forward as Flora and I swung the gate open.

"Do you suppose she's very ill?" Flora said as soon as the cart had rattled away up the hill. "Rose, I mean."

"I think she must be," I frowned. "Otherwise Arthur wouldn't have sent for the Doctor."

We stared at one another gloomily. The only time I could ever remember the Doctor being called for Flora and me was when we had the whooping cough.

"I wonder what it can be?" Flora said. I shook my head.

"I expect Arthur's telling Nellie more about it now that we're not there." Flora nodded.

"That's why they made us get out and walk. And did you notice? Nellie didn't say a word all the way. That's a sure sign she's worried."

"Perhaps she's afraid that whatever Rose has may be catching," I said.

"Goodness," Flora exclaimed, standing stock still and staring at me. "William – how awful. Supposing it is – catching. Do you know I'm beginning to feel quite funny already. Oh, I wish we hadn't come." I was wishing the same thing myself, but it didn't do any good to say so.

"It may not be as bad as we think," I told her, beginning to swing the gate shut.

At that moment we heard the sound of wheels behind us, and round the corner appeared a smart pony trap, going at a good lick, and with a sturdy bay pony between the shafts. Sitting on the box was an elderly man wearing a black coat and a bowler hat. Barely pausing to rein in the pony, he lifted his whip to us both and as Flora leapt nimbly to one side he shot through the open gate and up the hill towards The Cott.

"Did you see that?" Flora gasped. "He could have run me down – "

"It's the Doctor," I cut in, staring after him. "I'm sure it is."

"How do you know?" Flora asked.

38

"He just looked like a Doctor," I frowned. "Besides, he had a black bag on the seat beside him . . . the kind they always carry." We looked at one another. "Come on," I said, shutting the gate with a crash. "We'd better go and find out what's happening."

The Cott was further away than I'd thought, and it was uphill all the way. To begin with we ran, not bothering to stop and look at Arthur's donkeys grazing in the fields, although they lifted their heads to gaze at us as we raced by. But the hill grew steeper half way up, so that we both had to slow down to catch our breath, and then I got a stone in my boot which meant undoing all the laces before I could tip it out. By the time we arrived the Doctor had been there for some time. The bay pony stood outside, cropping the grass, his reins hitched over the gate post.

Nellie heard us coming and met us at the front door.

"The Doctor's 'ere," she said. "'E's waiting ter see yer. Wipe them boots and come inside."

Flora and I glanced at one another. Nellie was looking more subdued than ever, and not even stopping to sweep the bits of straw from Flora's skirt she hurried us into the cottage without another word.

We found ourselves in a low, whitewashed room with a red brick floor covered with rag rugs. A bright fire was burning in the range, and on the opposite wall was a dresser with blue and white china arranged on it, and propped up in the middle a picture of Queen Victoria. There was no sign of Arthur, so I guessed he must be upstairs with Rose, but standing beside the table with his bag in one hand and his hat in the other, stood the Doctor.

"So these are the two scallywags, eh?" he said, nodding to us. He was taller than I'd supposed, and very clean looking with a neat little grey beard and moustache.

"Yes, Sir," Nellie said. "This is Flora and William, Mr Samuel Rolandson's wards – like I told you."

"Come over here to the light then, and let's take a look at you," the Doctor said. "I've seen you already, haven't I?" He went on as Nellie propelled us forwards. "Down by the gate."

I saw Flora begin to open her mouth to tell him that he'd nearly knocked her over, but before she could speak he gave a quick nod and looked at Nellie.

"They seem like a sensible enough pair to me," he said. "Both got your heads screwed on pretty tight, eh? And ready to do what you can to help? Yes, I'm sure you are," he continued without waiting for an answer. "Nellie here was worrying about you, but I can see there's no need for that." I frowned, and Flora opened her mouth to ask what he meant, only once again the Doctor was too quick for her. "I daresay you're both wondering what all this is about," he nodded. "So – with your permission." He glanced over our heads towards Nellie, who was still standing behind us.

"It's best you tell them, Doctor," I heard her say.

"Nellie is going to be very busy for a while," he said, looking from one to the other of us. "Mrs Watkins is ill, you see. Quite ill . . ." He paused for a moment, his head cocked to one side, and this time Flora cut in.

"She is going to get better, isn't she?"

"Oh most certainly she is," the Doctor said. "I'm going to see to that. But it will take some time. You see, she has pneumonia, and that means she's going to need a great deal of looking after. Plenty of good nursing and special food to eat. Nellie will have her hands full for a while."

There was silence for a moment or two. Flora was staring down at her boots and trying to work out whether pneumonia was catching. But I could see the quiet, steady way the Doctor was looking at us both, and I knew in a flash what he was trying to tell us. I shot a quick glance over my shoulder at Nellie, just to make sure I was right. Then I took a deep breath.

"You're going to send us back to London again, aren't you?" I said.

CHAPTER FOUR

In which a telegram is dispatched, and Flora and I set out on a journey . . .

Flora's head came up with a jerk and she shot a quick look first at me and then at the Doctor.

"Go back to London without Nellie, you mean?"

"Back to your Guardian," the Doctor nodded.

"But we couldn't possibly do that," Flora exclaimed, suddenly turning very pink. "It wouldn't be fair."

"Fair?"

"We couldn't leave Nellie here alone," Flora said, shaking her head. "Could we, William?"

"Not even if it was for the best?" The Doctor enquired, raising his eyebrows a little and looking across at Nellie.

"But you don't want us to go, do you?" Flora demanded, turning to Nellie and taking her hand. "I mean, pneumonia's not catching, is it? And if we stayed we could help you." Nellie's face started to crinkle up and she gave Flora a quick kiss on the forehead, but she didn't speak.

Of course I didn't want to leave Nellie either, but I could see by the look on her face that the whole thing had already been decided, and it would only upset her more than ever if we kept on arguing, so when Flora turned to me I just shook my head.

"I think the Doctor's right," I told her. "If Nellie's got to stay here and look after Rose we'll only be in the way. Don't you see?"

Nellie shot me a quick, warm look and then squeezed Flora's hand.

"I know yer don't want ter go," she said. "And I don't want ter lose yer. But wot William says is true. We must do wot the Doctor thinks is best for Rose . . . and if Samuel wos 'ere I reckon 'e'd say the same."

That settled it. Samuel is always the final authority in our family, and although Flora still looked pretty doubtful, she had finally subsided into silence.

"I daresay it won't be for so very long," Nellie went on. "And the three of yer will just 'ave ter manage without me. I've got ter stay 'ere and look after Rose. Yer do understand that, don't yer?"

"Of course we do," I said quickly, and after a moment Flora nodded.

"Good – well that's arranged then," the Doctor said, settling his bowler hat on his head with an air of relief. "First train in the morning, eh?"

"Yes, Sir," Nellie said. "And yer won't forget, will yer?"

"No, no. You can rely on me," he replied tapping his pocket.

"Forget what?" I asked.

"The Doctor's goin' ter stop off in the village and send Samuel a telegram," Nellie said. "We wrote it out before yer got up 'ere."

"So your Guardian will be at the station to meet you when you reach London," the Doctor said. "Well – goodbye to you both, and no more worries about Mrs Watkins, eh? Nellie and I will see to it that she's back on her feet before long." He picked up his bag and went towards the door. "I'll be back to see her first thing in the morning," he added as he went. Nellie followed him out and Flora and I were left alone.

"I don't want to go a bit," Flora said in a low voice. "It still seems dreadful. Poor Nellie . . . how do you suppose she'll manage without us?"

"She'll have Arthur," I said. "And I expect she'll be too busy taking care of Rose to notice that we're not here." Flora gave me a quick, sideways look. I don't think she much liked the idea of Nellie not missing us. "Anyway," I went on, "they'd decided the whole thing while we were still walking up the hill. Nellie had even written out the telegram. So we've got to go."

At that moment we heard Arthur's footsteps creaking across the bedroom floor overhead, which made us both look up at the ceiling.

"Poor Rose," Flora said, giving a sudden shiver. "I'm glad I'm not ill in bed, aren't you, William?"

As nothing happened for the rest of that day I will skip over it, except to say that the time crawled by very slowly indeed. Arthur and Nellie took it in turns to sit with Rose, and even when they weren't at her bedside they were bustling in and out with hot water and towels and fresh coals for the fire, so neither of them had the time to pay much attention to us. We explored the garden and walked down the lane to see the donkeys, but then it began to rain so we had to go back to the cottage, and after that there was nothing to do except talk to the cat and remember to keep our voices down and not make any noise because of disturbing Rose. We had cold meat and pickles for supper, and at nine o'clock Nellie sent Arthur to tell us it was time for bed. By then we were so dejected that neither of us raised any objection, but followed him without a word as he led the way up the creaking staircase and along the passage.

It was Arthur who put his head round the door the next morning, too, telling us it was time to get up.

"I suppose Nellie's with Rose," Flora said as we struggled into our clothes in the grey, early morning light. "William, you'll have to help me with my buttons. I can't reach the back ones, no matter how hard I try."

But Nellie was downstairs by the time we got there, buttering bread and ladling out porridge as though her life depended on it.

She didn't give us time to ask how Rose was before she told us to sit down and eat up because Arthur had gone to fetch the donkey cart round and we'd have to leave in a quarter of an hour.

"Aren't you going to have any breakfast?" Flora asked.

"I'll 'ave something later, when you've gone," Nellie said, throwing the ladle back into the porridge pot. "I ain't got time now – there's things I must tell yer both."

"What things?" I asked, looking at Flora. "You didn't have any dinner yesterday either."

"Or any supper last night," Flora cut in, giving Nellie a worried look. "You'll get ill, too, if you don't eat."

"Flora's right," I said. Nellie stared at us both for a moment and then shut her mouth up tight and jabbed at a hair pin. But instead of getting angry, she suddenly gave a quick nod and pulling out a chair plumped herself down beside us at the table.

"Yer quite right," she said. "Both of yer. The truth is I 'ates ter see yer go off like this, yer 'oliday all spoilt and poor Rose so ill . . ."

"Isn't she any better this morning?" Flora asked. Nellie shook her head.

"Not a bit," she said. "So I've got ter stay 'ere and look after 'er, and I 'ope yer both understands." She looked from one to the other of us.

"Of course we do," I said. "You don't have to worry about us."

"Only we'll worry about you if we think you're not eating," Flora said.

"Well we can't 'ave that, can we?" Nellie said, screwing up her face and giving Flora a quick pat on the cheek. "Tell you wot – I'll 'ave a bit of bread and butter with some of that plum jam of Rose's on it . . . and you can pour me a cup of tea, William."

At that moment we heard the sound of wheels on the gravel outside.

"There now – that'll be Arthur with the donkey cart," Nellie said. "Now listen, both of yer, you in particular, William, 'cos I'm puttin' you in charge." She fished in her apron pocket and pulled out three letters and her purse. "'Ere's a letter for Samuel wot says more than the telegram did, so I want you to give it to 'im as soon as yer see 'im. And 'ere's two more letters to me other sisters – 'er wot lives near St Paul's and Grace in Brighton. But you'll 'ave to ask Samuel for stamps for them two 'cos I ain't got none. You will make sure they gets posted today, won't yer?"

"I promise," I said.

"And 'ere's yer return tickets, so don't lose them. Put them in yer pocket now. Yer won't really need no money 'cos Samuel will meet yer, but 'ere's 'alf a crown, just in case."

"I hope there's not a lot else to say, because time's running short," Arthur said from the doorway, as Nellie paused for breath. Flora and I scraped back our chairs and began putting on our hats and coats, while Nellie spread the slices of bread and butter with plum jam and turned them into sandwiches to eat on the journey. Then she hugged us both several times and told us to be good and take care of one another and not to be a trouble to Samuel, and that she'd write in a day or so to let us know how Rose was getting on. She was still standing at the open door waving to us as we rattled away in the donkey cart.

It seemed odd to be leaving Nellie behind and driving to the station to catch the train not knowing when we'd see her again. It would be odd, too, when we arrived home. Somehow Nellie was always there, whenever we came in or went out or got up in the morning or sat down to meals. But now, for the first time in our lives, we were going to be in the house without her. Of course Samuel would be there. And so, perhaps, would Chang. I glanced at Flora, but she was bent double, re-lacing one of her boots.

"I'm right sorry things had to turn out like this," Arthur said when we reached the station and were waiting on the platform for the train to arrive. "Rose and I was looking forward to your visit.

If I'd have known she was so ill I'd have telegraphed you not to come."

"It was a good thing we did come, though," Flora said sensibly. "Otherwise Nellie wouldn't have been here to look after Rose."

"Well that's right enough," Arthur nodded. "And I hopes you'll both come again. In the summer maybe. The Cott's the prettiest place in the world in summer." He sighed, and then stared along the line as though he'd run out of things to say. I could see that he really wanted to be off, but didn't like to leave without making sure we were on the train, and I was just going to tell him that it would be all right when we heard the signal go up, and the distant sound of the engine.

"Here she comes," he said, picking up the bags and looking quite relieved.

Flora and I were both pretty relieved, too, and although we shook hands and said goodbye as politely as possible and waved through the window to Arthur as the train steamed out, once he'd disappeared from view and we were really on our own I suddenly felt quite fizzy with excitement, as though I was a bottle of champagne and someone had just taken the cork out of me. I looked at Flora and grinned.

"Chuff-chuff . . . Chuff-chuff . . . Chuff-chuff-chuff . . ." I began.

"Diddley-doing . . . diddley-doing . . . diddley-doing . . ." Flora chimed in, taking off her gloves and throwing her hat wildly up into the rack. We went on for some time until the rhythm of the engine grew faster and faster, so that we couldn't keep up, and then we collapsed in helpless giggles and rolled about on the seats.

I suppose it was the relief of not having to whisper any more or be on our best behaviour so as not to disturb Rose.

"It's just as well we've got the carriage to ourselves," I said at last.

"And just as well Nellie can't see us," Flora nodded. Then she suddenly grew serious. "Won't it be strange at home without her? I suppose I'll have to do the cooking." She frowned. "The trouble is I can't make many things, except toast and scrambled eggs."

"We'll manage," I said. "I'll be in charge of the range if you like." I did my best to look as though I was making a noble gesture, but Flora wasn't taken in.

"Even when it goes out?" She asked innocently.

"It won't go out," I told her. "I'm very good at looking after it, only Nellie won't ever let me."

"We'll have to do everything we can to help Samuel," Flora went on solemnly. "It's going to be very different for a while, isn't it? Especially if Chang is still staying there."

As the train drew nearer to London we both became more and more serious. I pulled the tickets out of my pocket several times, just to make certain they were both still there, while Flora tidied her hair and put on her hat and gloves and picked imaginary bits of fluff off her skirt, just as though Nellie was actually there to tell her to do it, instead of miles away at The Cott. By the time the train drew to a halt at London Bridge Station I had got the bags down from the rack and was feeling quite excited at the thought of seeing Samuel.

We climbed out of the carriage, pulling the luggage after us, and began looking for him. Samuel is tall, and he always wears a large, black Fedora hat which makes him stand out in a crowd. There was no sign of him, though.

"I can't see him yet, can you?" Flora said, staring up and down the platform.

"He's probably waiting at the barrier," I said. All the other passengers had gone by then, and we were left, standing alone with the luggage. "Let's go and see."

We picked up our bags and began to walk up the platform, peering anxiously ahead for Samuel's tall, familiar figure. But when we arrived at the barrier and handed in our tickets there was no longer any doubt about it. Samuel was not there.

"What can have happened to him?" Flora said, letting her bag drop to the ground with a thump. "Samuel's never late." She stared anxiously around her and then looked at me. "You don't suppose that anything could have gone wrong, do you?"

"Perhaps he thought we were coming on a later train," I said.

"Perhaps that Doctor didn't send the telegram at all," Flora said doubtfully. "And if he didn't – then Samuel won't know we're coming home."

I looked at her. I was beginning to have a nasty, sinking feeling in the pit of my stomach.

"Doctor's don't forget important things like that," I said, shaking my head. "You wait here. I'm going to find out when the next train comes in."

But there wasn't another train from Rochester until two o'clock that afternoon.

"What are we going to do?" Flora said, when I came back and told her. "Half a crown may not be enough for a hansom, and we can't possibly walk all the way home. It's miles."

"Look," I said, suddenly remembering the two sovereigns that Samuel had given me just before we left. I pulled them out of my inside pocket and showed her. "Come on, let's go and find one. Even if Samuel thought we were coming on the later train he won't have left home. It's only half past ten." I pointed at the clock.

For a little while we felt more cheerful, and once we were in the hansom and driving towards Kennington we tried to imagine how surprised Samuel would be when he opened the door and saw us standing on the step.

"I'll go and ring the bell," Flora cried, bounding out of the hansom as soon as it drew up outside the house, and leaving me to haul out the bags and pay the driver.

"That'll be half a crown exactly, sir," the driver said. I knew

48

that Samuel always gave a tip, so I handed him one of the sovereigns instead of Nellie's half crown, and while I waited for the change I wondered how much to leave. Sixpence didn't seem quite enough, so in the end I made it a shilling.

"Thank you very kindly, sir," the driver said, touching his cap and putting the shilling in his pocket directly. "All right then?" He added. "You don't want me to wait, do you?"

"No, thank you," I said, thinking it a bit odd. But when I turned round I understood. Flora was still standing at the top of the steps, and the front door was still closed.

"All the windows are shut, too," she said, as I carried the bags up the path. "I noticed as soon as I got out of the cab. Samuel's not here, William. I've rung and rung – and we can't get in. Whatever shall we do?"

CHAPTER FIVE

In which we are puzzled by disappearances . . .

I stood and stared at the front door.

"He must be there," I said. Flora shook her head.

"He isn't," she said.

"Perhaps he didn't hear you." I frowned, and seizing the bell pull I dragged at it as hard as I could several times. The jangling rose to a crescendo and then died away, and as the silence echoed around us again I had to admit that Flora was right. Wherever Samuel was at that moment he certainly wasn't at home.

"I expect he's gone to buy something for lunch," I muttered, still unable to believe that he was far away. I turned and looked up and down the street, half expecting to see his familiar figure rounding the corner and striding towards us whistling Pop Goes the Weasel. But there was nobody in sight. Even the cabbie had disappeared.

"It's Sunday," Flora said in a small voice. "The shops aren't open. William, what are we going to do?"

A thin, grey drizzle had begun to fall, wetting the cobblestones and the black iron railings in front of the houses. I looked at Flora and saw that her eyes had filled with tears.

"Don't," I said. "Please don't cry. We'll think of something . . ."

"I'm sorry," she gulped. "I know you hate it when I cry, and I am trying not to . . . honestly I am . . ." She wiped her sleeve across her face.

"The kitchen door might be open," I said desperately.

I ran down the steps and pushed open the black iron gate that led into the area. But the kitchen door was locked, and bolted inside, too, I thought, because it didn't budge or rattle when I put my shoulder to it.

"I knew it wouldn't be any use," Flora said as I came up the steps again. She sat down on her portmanteau and buried her face in her hands. I stared at her helplessly for a moment, wondering what to do next. And then I had an idea.

"Come on," I said, grabbing her by the arm and pulling her up. "I've thought of something . . ."

"What?" She said.

"It might not work, but at least it's better than sitting on the front door step just waiting." I began to run.

I raced around the corner and turned into the narrow lane which runs all the way along the back of our row of houses. On one side of the lane there is a wall, with gates in it leading into the back gardens. Our gate is locked from inside, but I thought we might be able to climb over the wall, and from there I was pretty certain we'd manage to get in through the wash house window. It doesn't close properly and Nellie's always complaining about the draught that whistles through it in the winter. If we could only get into the house then at least we'd be able to find something to eat and sit by the kitchen range while we waited for Samuel to come home.

"This isn't any good," Flora said, catching up with me as I reached the back gate. "You know Nellie keeps it locked." For a moment I didn't answer. I was staring up at the wall, but it was much higher than I remembered.

"If we had a ladder we could climb over," I said. "Suppose you stood on my shoulders." Flora shook her head.

"There's bits of glass and spikes all the way along the top," she said. "To keep the cats out. Anyway I couldn't jump from there to the garden. It's much too far."

"Well, that's that then," I said gloomily. "We'll just have to sit

51

outside and wait until Samuel gets back." It had begun to rain quite heavily by then. There were puddles all around our feet and up and down the lane. I stared furiously at the gate and then gave it a final, ferocious kick with my boot.

"William!" Flora cried. "Look!" To our astonishment the gate had opened and as we watched it swung slowly back on its hinges with a creak. For a moment we stared at one another.

"Nellie must have forgotten to lock it," I said. "What a bit of luck!" Then we both made a dive through the gate.

The wash house is a longish, low building that sticks out at right angles from the back of the house, beyond the scullery. Beside it is the outhouse where Samuel keeps the doves which he uses in his magic act. As Flora and I raced down the garden path we could see the doves through the window, coo-ing and fluttering in their cages, and the sight of them made me feel suddenly more cheerful. Samuel must have gone in to feed them that morning, I thought, just as he always did, and whatever else happened he would be there to feed them in the evening. The doves are all snow white, and they're quite valuable, being trained to do what Samuel wants them to during the performance. That's why he always feeds them himself and spends some time each day talking to them and handling them, so that they're quite used to him and recognise the sound of his voice. The only time they leave their cages is when Samuel takes them to the theatre, and sometimes, on Sundays, early in the morning, when we take them to the park and then let them fly back home. They always do fly home. Doves have a very strong homing instinct and Samuel's never lost one yet.

Flora closed her eyes tightly and crossed her fingers when we got to the wash house, and I shot a quick look at the window and grinned. It's a sash window, and very small. A full grown man or woman couldn't possibly squeeze through it, but I reckoned that Flora would be able to, and I could see that the latch, which was meant to hold the top and bottom sashes together, wasn't pulled across.

"You can open your eyes," I told her. "It's going to be all right."

To begin with we tried pushing the bottom sash upwards, but although we could reach it quite easily it was too stiff to move.

"There's an old stool by the washing line," Flora said. "If you stood on that perhaps you could pull the top bit down."

Flora held the stool steady while I climbed up on to it. By then my hands were wet and they kept slipping as I tried to get a grip on the wooden rib that ran down the middle of the window. But at last, after a lot of tugging, I felt it move a little so that I was able to get my fingers over the top of the frame, and with a final heave the window gave a groan and juddered down.

"You've done it!" Flora cried, clapping wildly and forgetting all about the stool, so that I nearly overbalanced and had to grab the window to steady myself.

"Do you think you can squeeze through there?" I asked, as we surveyed the window. "You're smaller than me." Flora looked doubtfully at the gap.

"It's not very big, is it?" she said. "Supposing I get stuck."

"You'll have to try," I told her. "We can't go on standing here – we're getting soaked to the skin. Come on, I'll give you a leg up." I helped her on to the stool and held it steady. I could feel the rain trickling down the back of my neck as Flora began to ease herself gingerly through the gap. She had got one leg through and was half way over when she stopped.

"Go on," I urged her.

"It's all very well for you," she said in a muffled voice. "I'm not sure if I can do it . . . there's nothing to hang on to."

"Well jump then," I told her. "You look awfully funny from here – all legs and petticoats and drawers." That did it. The next moment she had jumped and I heard her land with a crash on the wash house floor. "Are you all right?" I asked.

"I think so," she said. "I've banged my elbow ... Owch! And my skirt's torn too ..."

"Never mind that," I said. "Just go up and open the front door. The spare key is beside the clock. I'll come round and wait for you."

I raced back up the garden path, feeling rather pleased with myself. Now that I knew we weren't going to have to spend the afternoon waiting on the door step for Samuel I was thinking how surprised he'd be when he arrived home and found us in the house.

As I came round the corner I could see Flora waiting for me at the front door. Even before I realised what she was holding in her hand I knew that something was wrong.

"What is it?" I asked. She didn't answer, but held out the small, yellowish envelope for me to see. "The telegram," I frowned. "The one the Doctor sent ..." Flora nodded.

"It was on the front door mat with some other letters," she said. "And it hasn't been opened, William."

"No wonder Samuel wasn't at the station," I said slowly. "He doesn't even know that we've come back."

"There are other things, too," Flora went on in a frightened voice, following me into the hall and shutting the door. "The range is almost out. I don't think anyone's put any coal on it since yesterday. And the grandfather clock's stopped." I shot a quick glance at it and saw that the hands stood at half past eight. "Samuel always winds it on Sunday mornings," she said. "He never forgets."

She was still holding the telegram, and the rain water was dripping off the ends of her hair and making little splashes on the polished boards at her feet. As we stood there the stillness seemed to echo around us. I wished, more than anything, that Nellie was there, rattling the range, or clattering tea cups; or that Samuel would come out of the drawing room, whistling. But nothing happened.

"It's worse than ever, isn't it?" Flora said in a shaky voice.

I took the telegram from her and tore it open.

REGRET TO SAY ROSE VERY ILL STOP PLEASE MEET WILLIAM AND FLORA ARRIVING LONDON BRIDGE STATION TEN THIRTY STOP WRITING STOP LOVE NELLIE

I had suddenly begun to shiver with cold. My trousers were so wet they were sticking to my legs. Flora was soaked too, and her face was all streaked with dirt. She took the telegram from me.

"At least we managed to get in," I said after a moment. Flora nodded.

"Your teeth are chattering," she said, in an empty voice.

"It's because I'm cold," I told her. "If Nellie was here she'd tell us both to go and get out of our wet clothes, wouldn't she?" I tried to smile, but it didn't really work. Flora swallowed.

"We could pretend," she said. "Pretend that she is here, and that Samuel's going to be back in half an hour and we have to get ready for him. We could have a kind of race . . . put on dry clothes and make up the range. Lay the table – "

"I'm not very hungry," I said.

"I expect you are really," Flora said obstinately. "So hungry that you don't know it. That happens sometimes. And then, if Samuel does come back soon, he'll be pleased with everything we've done."

"It's only pretending, though, isn't it?" I said, staring at the telegram which Flora was still holding. "Because Nellie's not here – "

"I know," Flora cut in fiercely. "But swear it all the same." She dropped the telegram on to the hall chair.

"All right," I nodded after a moment.

"Honour Bright that you'll do it properly."

"Honour Bright," I said. We both licked our fingers and drew them across our throats to seal the pledge.

Once we'd sworn we had to stick to it, which was a good thing, because otherwise we might have gone on sitting around in our wet clothes getting colder and colder, and anyway the range would have gone out.

As soon as we'd changed we went downstairs to the kitchen, and while Flora laid the table with all that she could find in the larder I set about coaxing the range back to life, opening up all the dampers and feeding it with little shovels of coal until it was blazing brightly again. When we'd eaten some of the cold game pie and pickles and cheese, and several pieces of bread and marmalade and were feeling more cheerful, Flora pushed back her chair, and after licking her fingers announced that the half hour must be up by now so we could stop pretending.

"I believe that Samuel's gone away," she added, in such a calm, matter of fact way that I put down my knife and stared at her.

"He can't have done," I frowned.

"Then why didn't he open the telegram?" I couldn't answer that, and for a moment I didn't say anything. "And it's not just the telegram," she went on. "I've had a funny feeling all along – ever since we got off the train."

"One of your hunches, you mean?" She nodded.

"When I rang the door bell and no one answered, I knew what was going to happen. That was why I cried, I suppose. The worst part was coming into the house and seeing that the clock had stopped. Everything seemed so quiet and empty . . ." She stopped for a moment and bit her lip. "I don't feel so bad about it any more. Not now. Only I'm not quite sure what we're going to do."

I scraped back my chair and went and put another shovel full of coal on the fire while I tried to think. Somewhere at the back of my mind a thought was jigging about. I frowned, and then, suddenly I remembered.

"He can't have gone away," I said, throwing the shovel back into the coal scuttle and turning round. "What about the doves?"

"I've thought of that," Flora said.

"Well then? You know that Samuel would never go away unless he'd arranged for them to be looked after," I said.

"That's just it," Flora nodded, running her finger round the top of the marmalade jar. "You said yourself that the back gate was always locked." I stared at her blankly. "Don't you see? Samuel must have arranged for someone to come in that way and feed them while he's gone. That was why it was open."

I saw then that she was right. We were quite alone. Just Flora and me in the empty house.

"He might not be back for days," I said slowly. "As far as he knows we're down at The Cott with Nellie." Flora nodded solemnly.

"And the worst part of it is that we don't have the least idea where he is," she said.

I stared at the faded colours in the rag rug under my feet and my mind raced back over all that had happened since Friday evening. There were so many things that seemed odd, right from the moment when we'd first seen the letter sitting on the hall chair. Chang's arrival, and the unaccountable way that Samuel had behaved, only letting us into the drawing room for ten minutes; Chang himself, sitting in the wing chair in the shadows. And then the other Chinese man. I hadn't thought about him all day, but now the memory of him standing outside our house in the moonlight flooded back into my mind and I felt a prickle of fear run down my spine. I pushed the thought away and looked up. Flora was watching me.

"All this has got something to do with Chang," she said in a low voice.

"Do you think that, too?" I said. Flora nodded and leant forward.

"I thought the mystery was solved, but instead we seem to be right in the middle of it."

"They talked for hours after we'd gone to bed," I told her. "I could hear their voices."

"And now Samuel's vanished," Flora said. "William, what are we going to do? We can't go back to The Cott."

"If only we knew where he'd gone," I said. "And when he's coming back. Just to go away without telling us . . ."

"Or Nellie," Flora nodded. "She couldn't have had any idea or she'd never have sent us home today, no matter what that Doctor said. It must be something very important. And secret too . . . so secret that he couldn't even talk to us about it." I stared at the coals shifting behind the bars of the range, and frowned.

"Supposing he has written to us all, down there," I said. "Nellie will get the letter tomorrow, by the first post . . ."

We looked at one another, imagining how worried Nellie would be, and wondering whether she'd pack a bag and come straight back to London. Just for a moment I couldn't think what we ought to do.

"Where are you going?" Flora asked, watching me walk towards the door.

"Those letters Nellie gave me," I said. "For her sisters – I'd better go and post them."

"But the last post doesn't leave for hours," Flora said. "And we haven't decided anything yet."

"I promised," I said. "Besides, it'll give me a chance to think. When I get back we'll try to make a plan." Flora looked uneasily out of the window. It was only the middle of the afternoon, but it was already growing dark. "You'll be all right, won't you?" I asked, fiddling with the door knob. She tilted her chin.

"Of course I will," she said. "Oh, do go on, William, if you're going."

I could tell that she didn't really want to be left alone, even for five minutes, and I must admit that as I ran upstairs I was trying not to think about the two of us being all on our own in the empty house. Even your own home, which is as ordinary as rice pudding during the day can make you feel quite jumpy when there's no one there but you and it's beginning to get dark.

My jacket was lying in a crumpled heap on the hall floor where I'd thrown it, and the letters were rather damp when I pulled them out of the pocket. Nellie had addressed them with a lead pencil, which was lucky, because if it had been ink it might have smudged. I put the letter to Samuel on the hall chair beside the telegram and went upstairs.

Samuel keeps his stamps in one of the cubby holes of the desk in his bedroom, and as I turned the handle and opened the door I could see at once that the room had that tidy, clean-swept look which tells you that the owner isn't going to be back for some time. His bed was made and his sponge and shaving brush and razor had all gone from the wash stand. I wondered whether he had locked the desk, but the lid opened all right when I tried it. I took two stamps from the cubby hole and was just sticking them on the letters when I saw the photograph. It was propped up inside the desk and even in the fading light I could tell that it was quite old, because of the brownish tints in it. I picked it up curiously and went over to the window to have a closer look.

It must have been taken while Samuel was in India. There was a servant in a turban holding the horses' heads, and standing in front of a tent a group of four soldiers. One of them was Samuel. The two men next to him were standing quite close together with their arms linked, and a little apart was the fourth man. He was the tallest, but it was hard to see his face because he was half turned away from the camera, looking at the others. I've seen a great many photographs of Samuel as the Astonishing Rolandson, but I'd never seen a picture of him in his army uniform before, and I stood there by the window for about a minute before putting the photograph back inside the desk. Then I picked up the letters and went out.

There is a pillar box at the end of the street, so it didn't take me long to post the letters, especially as I ran all the way there and back. Being outside, with the wind and the rain blowing against my face helped me to think more clearly, and I'd made up my mind what we ought to do by the time I came back up the front steps. Somehow or other we must try to find Samuel. I even had an idea of where we might begin looking for him, and I wanted to tell Flora about it.

"It's me," I called. "I'm back." I took the stairs two at a time, wondering why she didn't answer, and bounded through the kitchen door.

"Listen," I said, "I've been thinking – " And then I stopped.

Flora was standing stock still in the middle of the kitchen holding the poker and staring at the scullery door.

"Flora . . ." I said.

"Ssh," she whispered, putting her finger to her lips, but still not moving her gaze from the door.

"What is it?" I whispered, my own heart beginning to pound against my ribs. It was so quiet that I could hear the distant sound of a hansom passing at the end of the street. "What's the matter?"

"A face," Flora breathed. "I saw a face at the window . . ."

"A face?" I frowned.

"I was taking the cheese out – to put it away, and when I turned round, there it was . . . looking at me through the scullery window."

"What sort of a face was it?" I asked, my mind beginning to race. "Was it a man?"

60

"No, it was a boy," Flora said. "At least I think so. He had a cap on that was too big for him and he was very white and . . ."

"Go on," I muttered. "And what?"

"Pinched looking," she said. "William, do you suppose he's still there?"

"I don't know," I said. "But I'm going to look."

"You can't," Flora said shaking her head violently. "No . . ."

"I'm not scared of a boy," I told her. "You can wait here if you like." I took the poker from her and opened the back door and peered out into the garden.

There was no one on the path and the gate was closed, but as I stared past the dripping laurel bushes towards the wall, I suddenly saw that something was wrong. Grasping the poker more firmly I began to run up the path.

The door of the dove house stood wide open, and when I got there and looked inside I saw that the wire cages were empty. The doves had gone.

CHAPTER SIX

In which we begin our search . . .

"Gone!" Flora gasped. "You mean – all gone?"

"All of them," I said, throwing the poker back into the coal scuttle with a clatter. "And the basket too." Flora stood and stared at me, her eyes growing as wide as saucers.

"Samuel's precious doves. . . . Stolen!" she whispered. "Then . . . that boy I saw . . . William! Quick, we must go after him."

"No," I said, catching hold of her arm.

"But we must. I'm going to even if you won't . . ."

"It's no use," I told her. "Stop whirling about like that and listen – "

"Let go of me," Flora panted, aiming a kick at my shins. "It'll be too late in a minute – "

"It's too late now," I shouted. "That's what I've been trying to tell you, only you won't listen. The back gate's locked and the key's gone. We can't get out that way – "

"The front door, then – " I shook my head.

"That's no good. We'd never catch him . . . he's probably miles away by now." I let go of her arm and sat down on Nellie's old rose patterned armchair.

"Samuel's precious, precious doves," Flora said again, staring at me and rubbing her arm. "Whatever will he do?" I looked up at her.

"You still don't understand, do you?" I said slowly. "How did he know where to find the key? And if he is a thief, then why did he bother to lock the gate after him?"

A look of bewildered astonishment crept over Flora's face as she tumbled to what I was saying.

"You mean – you think that Samuel sent him to fetch them?"

"He may have done," I nodded. "Of course we can't know for certain. But if he did then that boy might have told us where to find Samuel. If only I'd been here instead of posting those letters . . ."

I stopped. But it was too late. Flora was staring at me in dismay.

"It's all my fault, isn't it?" She said miserably. "I should have gone after him with the poker, like you did."

"It's different for boys," I said.

"No it isn't," Flora said, shaking her head. "I'm just a coward, that's all."

"What tosh!" I cut in. "You're braver than I am about lots of things – going to the dentist for instance. As a matter of fact I think you're very brave." Flora's face brightened a little. "Anyway, I expect I'd have been in a blue funk too if I'd seen him staring in at me through the window."

"It was horrible," Flora said with a shudder. "He looked like a goblin – a hobgoblin . . ."

"He didn't have a pigtail, did he?" I asked, just to make sure.

"No, I told you. He was wearing a cap." She frowned. "Like the one the butcher's boy wears. What made you think of a pigtail?"

"It doesn't matter," I said gruffly, jumping up and going over to the window. "He's gone now, anyway, and taken the doves with him." I frowned. "I wish we knew whether Samuel did send him – "

"I just wish that Samuel would come back," Flora broke in wildly. "We don't really know anything for certain, do we? And it keeps getting worse all the time."

It had grown much darker while we had been talking, and the lamplighter must have passed on his nightly round, because I could see the glow of the street lamp through the front window. Standing there in the darkened kitchen it seemed for a minute or two as though everything we'd always counted on had somehow crumbled away and vanished. I wanted to tell Flora that at least we still had one another, but I had a lump in my throat that made it difficult to speak, so I began looking for the matches instead.

"What are you doing?" Flora asked.

"No sense in sitting here in the dark," I muttered.

On winter evenings Nellie always lights the lamps at three o'clock, long before the lamplighter comes round. She hates either of us to interfere, and if we so much as touch the matches she gets quite sharp. But I'd watched her hundreds of times, so I knew exactly what to do. I lit a match and turned the gas up until it popped and then glowed into life, sending the shadows scurrying away into the corners. When I turned round the kitchen had taken on its own, ordinary, comfortable look again and suddenly everything else seemed clearer, too.

"We've got to find Samuel," I said. "It's more important than ever now."

"Now that the doves have gone, you mean," Flora nodded. "I've been thinking the same thing. But how, William, when we don't know where to look?"

"I've had an idea," I said. "I was going to tell you as soon as I got back from posting the letters . . ."

"Go on," Flora said.

"We could write to Gus," I said. "Or send her a telegram. We've still got plenty of money left. We could send it first thing in the morning."

"You don't think he's gone down there, do you?" Flora asked, looking at me doubtfully. Gus is Samuel's sister, and she lives in Cornwall.

"He might have done," I said. "And even if he's not there, Gus might come up and look after us, if she knew we were on our own. Just until Samuel gets back." I stopped. Flora was shaking her head.

"That's no use," she said. "I'm sure Samuel isn't there."

"How can you be so sure?" I asked. Flora wrinkled up her nose.

"Because he would have told us if he was going to stay with Gus. And anyway, I'm still quite certain that all this has got something to do with Chang." She was silent for a moment. Then, quite suddenly, she let out a great yelp.

"William! I've got it!" She cried. "The Alhambra! We'll go to the Alhambra."

"Hang on," I said, as Flora started to dance round the room. "Why the Alhambra? Samuel isn't even booked to appear there – "

"No, but Chang is," Flora said, waving her arms around excitedly. "Don't you see? If Chang's going to open there soon the Manager must know where he's staying – "

"Of course," I said slowly. "And Chang will tell us how to find Samuel." Flora nodded. "You know," I went on, shooting her an admiring glance, "that's a much better idea than mine. Not far short of brilliant."

Flora wriggled a little and then dropped me a mock curtsey.

"I think it's going to work," I grinned.

"All we have to do is wait until tomorrow morning, and then go to the theatre," Flora nodded. "We'll go first thing, won't we?"

"Straight after breakfast," I agreed.

Now that we had decided on a plan the hardest part was not being able to put it into action until the next day. We'd never spent a night on our own before, and although neither of us talked about it I knew that Flora was dreading it as much as I was. The time seemed to stretch ahead like a tunnel until the next morning, and the moment when we could set out to look for Samuel. Bed time was the worst part of all. I suppose that we'd both been hoping against hope that we might hear the sound of Samuel's key in the lock, but at last, when the hands of the kitchen clock had moved round to ten o'clock, and there was no sign of him, I stood up.

"I'll come and sleep in your room if you like," I said, not looking at Flora as I lit the oil lamp. "In Nellie's bed. Then I can help with your buttons and things . . ."

"Would you?" Flora said in a small voice.

"And we'll keep the lamp on low," I added. "Like when we're ill."

Fifteen minutes later we were in bed, and the last thing I can remember before I fell asleep was the comfortable glow of the oil lamp and the sound of the rain still beating against the window panes.

Flora was up and dressed before I woke up the next morning.

"We've done it," she announced, pulling back the curtains with a great whoosh so that a flood of sunshine poured into the room. "We've actually spent a whole night on our own, and we're still here and still alive. Do you know I don't believe I'll ever be frightened of anything ever again. Buttons, please," she added, sitting down heavily on my feet and turning her back so that I could do them up.

"What time is it?" I asked, heaving myself up in the bed and wishing, as I did very often, that Flora wasn't so horribly bright first thing in the mornings. I seemed to be all fingers and thumbs as I struggled with the buttons.

"Half past eight," she said. "I've been waiting for you to wake up for ages and then I couldn't wait any longer. I've put the kettle on and laid the table . . . and done the washing up from last night – "

"Is the range still alight?" I asked. "I hope you didn't fiddle with it."

"No, I left that for you," Flora said primly, over her shoulder. "Do hurry up, William. Nellie does them in half the time."

"It'd be easier if you kept still," I told her. "Anyway, that's the last one." She leapt off the bed and scooping her brush and comb off the top of the chest of drawers, made for the door. Then she stopped.

"I don't know what we'll do if we can't find Samuel," she said. "There isn't much food left – we ate such a lot last night. You are going to get up, aren't you?" I nodded.

"The sooner we get to the Alhambra the better," I said. "And don't touch the range," I shouted after her.

As soon as we'd had breakfast we set off. After the rain it was a bright, windy day, the sort that cheers you up, with plenty of white and grey clouds racing across a blue sky and drifts of fallen leaves in the gutters and whisking along the pavements. We found a cab as soon as we reached the corner, and Flora climbed in while I told the driver we wanted to go to the Alhambra Theatre. I jingled the half crowns in my pocket as I spoke, so that he'd know we had the money to pay him. It seemed easy enough, as we set off, to push the nagging doubts to the back of my mind. By midday, I thought, we would be with Samuel.

"Just imagine," Flora said, wriggling to the edge of the seat so that she could look out of the window, "this is the third time in three days that we've been in a hansom, and the second time we've been in one on our own." I looked out of the other window, trying to think things over. "I've decided," Flora went on, "as soon as we've found Samuel and all this is over I'm going to write Nellie a long letter to cheer her up. Imagine how surprised she'll be when she finds out that we spent a whole night on our own."

The playbills outside the Alhambra had Chang's name written on them.

"Listen to this," Flora said, as soon as I'd paid the cab driver and joined her at the doors. " 'We are proud to announce,' " she read, " 'for the very first time in London, and all the way from the Mysterious Orient – ' "

"That's not true," I cut in, "he's come from America – "

"'Chang,'" Flora went on, waving to me to be quiet, and declaiming so dramatically that several passers by stopped and stared at us. "'The Greatest Magician the World has ever seen. . . . Never again will you experience such Stupefaction and Wonder. . . . Never again – '"

"Flora," I hissed, seizing her by the wrist and dragging her away. "Come on."

"But I've only got half way," she protested. "And the best bits were just coming."

"We've got to find the Manager," I told her, pushing the door into the foyer open.

"He won't be here anyway," Flora said in such a definite way that I stopped and looked at her. "Not in the front of house. We'll have to go round to the stage door. Follow me," she said, giving a little toss of her head. When it comes to anything to do with theatres Flora seems to have a kind of instinct, and as she's generally right I let her lead the way round the side of the theatre and up a narrow alleyway.

The stage door was ajar, and sitting just inside, in a dimly lit cubby hole, was the Stage Door Keeper. He was old, like most stage door keepers, and he wore an ancient checked cap and mittens, and a knitted silk muffler which had once been white. On a stool in front of him was a wedge of bread and dripping and a glass of beer.

"Good morning," Flora said, putting both hands on the counter and giving him one of her best smiles. "We'd like to see the Manager."

"Would you now," the man said, in a voice that was half a wheeze and half a growl.

"If you please, that is," Flora nodded, suddenly remembering her manners. The Stage Door Keeper looked us both up and down. Then he pulled out a vast, red spotted handkerchief and blew his nose. We waited.

68

"There's many as would like to see him, I reckon," he said at last, putting the handkerchief back in his pocket. It isn't often that one of Flora's smiles meets with such a stony response, and I could see that at any moment he was going to tell us to go away. She shot me a baffled look.

"Could you tell us if the Manager's here," I said, stepping forward. "It's very important." The Stage Door Keeper looked from Flora to me and gave a knowing nod.

"I'll tell you something, son," he said, leaning forward confidentially. "It always is."

"But it is," Flora cut in. "It really and truly is."

"There you are, you see," the man nodded, giving a wheezy chuckle and winking at me. "Never knew a time when it wasn't. I'll tell you something else," he went on. "Even if Mr Morton was here, and I'm not saying that he is, mind . . . he don't see young persons without an appointment. Chances are you'd be wasting his time, and Mr Morton's a very busy man." Flora and I looked at one another.

"I believe he thinks we want an engagement in the Pantomime," she whispered.

"All parts are cast in this year's Pantomime," he said, over his shoulder. "I told you, you're wasting your time."

"But we don't want parts in the Pantomime," I said desperately. "Look, is the Manager here or not? It really is very urgent."

The man gave a huge, wheezy sigh, and then pulled a stub of pencil out from behind his ear.

"Name," he said. "And nature of business." Flora put her hands on the counter.

"I'm Flora," she said, "And this is William. But – "

"Rolandson," I cut in.

"Rolandson, eh?" The man said slowly. "Rolandson, did you say?" Only this time I saw that his expression had changed, and he looked at us both curiously. "No connection with Samuel Roland-son, I daresay?"

"Of course there is," I said, straightening my shoulders. "He's our Guardian."

"You should 'ave said so in the first place," the man said, pushing the pencil back behind his ear again and lumbering to his feet.

"Do you know Samuel, then?" Flora asked.

"I know everyone, and everyone knows me," he said. "Fred, that's my name. Used to be at the Holborn Empire before I came 'ere." He had suddenly grown very affable and was shaking us both by the hand. "I remember you, young sir," he went on, "when you used ter be put ter sleep in a property basket . . . must be all of ten years ago. Yer've grown a bit since them days."

At the mention of the Holborn Empire Flora had grown quite pink, because of course that was the theatre in which Samuel had opened the box that was meant to contain a white rabbit, and found her inside instead. At any moment I could tell that she'd be asking Fred if he remembered it, and getting him to tell her the story all over again. So before she could begin I cut in quickly.

"Now that you know who we are," I said, "couldn't you let us see Mr Morton at once? You see, we're trying to find someone urgently and we're sure Mr Morton must know where he is."

"Who is it you're looking for?" Fred asked.

"Chang," I said.

"Chang?" Fred's eyebrows rose half an inch and he leant forward over the counter.

"You know," Flora interrupted. "The Greatest Magician in the World. His name's on all the bills outside."

"I know all right," Fred said.

"And have you any idea where we could find him?" I asked.

"Only arrived in London last week – from America, I believe," Fred said slowly. "And booked hisself into the Dukes Hotel . . ."

"Dukes," Flora exclaimed.

"Pall Mall," Fred nodded.

"Oh thank you, thank you," Flora cried. "Now we don't need to see the Manager at all, do we, William? We can go round there at once." But I had been watching Fred's face.

"Hang on a minute, Flora," I said as she started to go to the door.

"What for?" She tugged at my arm. "Come on, William, we're just wasting time."

"I don't think so," I said. I looked at Fred.

"Yer brother's right," he said. "No sense in going round to Dukes, 'cos the great Chang ain't there. The fact is – " He paused, looking from one to the other of us.

"Go on," I said. "Please – "

"I don't rightly know whether I ought to tell you this, but seeing as you're both in the business near enough, I suppose there's no harm . . . only yer won't go blabbing about it, now will yer? Or you'll get me into trouble."

"We know how to keep a secret," I said. Fred nodded.

"The truth is," he said, lowering his voice, "there's a bit of a hullabaloo going on about the Great Chang. You're not the only people as wants to see him. Mr Morton's gone looking for him too. Searching high and low, as you might say. No one's seen the gent since Friday last, and if 'e's not found soon the Alhambra's going to be in trouble." Flora and I looked at one another. "The fact is," said Fred, shaking his head with gloomy relish, "the Great Chang has vanished."

CHAPTER SEVEN

In which there are callers at the house, and we follow the whiff of oysters . . .

It was like walking into a brick wall, or turning a somersault and finding that the world was suddenly the wrong way up. We had been so certain that we would find Chang that morning, and be with Samuel by midday. But Chang had disappeared too, and now it seemed as though we were further than ever from discovering where Samuel had gone.

Flora had followed me down the alleyway and we were standing outside the front of the Alhambra where the bill boards announced Chang's opening.

"I think we should have waited," she said, looking at me anxiously and twisting her tam o'shanter round in her hands. "Fred told us he'd be back in a minute, and you could see he wanted to help – "

"How could he help?" I said. "He doesn't know where Chang is."

"Perhaps if we told him everything . . ." Flora began.

She looked back over her shoulder towards the stage door. A man selling roasted chestnuts had trundled his brazier down the street and was setting it up outside the theatre. I watched him for a moment, trying to decide what we ought to do next and suddenly feeling afraid. I had that sinking feeling in the pit of my stomach that you get just before you're going to the dentist.

"I think we should go back," Flora said. I shook my head. "But why not, William? He was nice in the end – as soon as he realised about Samuel being our Guardian . . ."

"He'll ask a lot of questions, though, won't he?" I said. "And he'll realise that we're alone, and that there's no one to look after us. And then he'll have to do something . . . take charge of us . . ."

I saw the sudden, fearful look on Flora's face and I knew that the same thought was in both our minds; the spectre that had haunted us ever since we could remember.

"The Workhouse," she whispered. "Oh William, whatever shall we do if anything's happened to Samuel?"

"Nothing's happened to him," I said gruffly. "We don't know where he is, that's all."

"He will come back, won't he?" Flora said, suddenly catching hold of my arm.

"Of course he will," I told her.

We both knew in our heart of hearts that Samuel would never abandon us. But now that Chang had mysteriously vanished as well, Samuel's absence seemed more bewildering than ever.

"Look," I said after a moment, "we can't talk about it here, in the street like this. We'd better go home." We had been standing outside the Alhambra for some time and a commissionaire was eyeing us curiously from inside the foyer. Flora nodded.

"You never know," she said as we moved off, "Samuel might be there when we get home." I didn't answer. "Shall we take a cab or go by tram?" She took my arm and glanced over her shoulder at the line of hansoms waiting on the other side of the street. I pulled out what was left of the money and counted it. There was one pound, nineteen shillings. "Plenty for a cab, isn't there?" Flora said, watching me.

"Suppose something happens and we absolutely have to take a hansom," I said, frowning.

"What sort of thing?" Flora asked.

"Or send a telegram. A tram's only tuppence from here . . . we can take a thirty three."

"But we'll probably have to wait for ages," Flora objected.

"No, we won't," I told her. "There's one coming now. We can catch it if we run."

Once we were on board Flora appeared to forget all about Samuel and Chang and the awful mess we were in, and struck up a conversation almost at once with a large, red-faced woman and her red-faced baby, googling and coo-ing over it in a pretty disgusting way and fluttering her eyelashes at the woman. She can be quite embarrassing sometimes when we're out together, and I watched her out of the corner of my eye and did my best to pretend that we weren't related. I was glad that we had taken a tram instead of a hansom, because the journey took longer, and more than anything I was dreading the moment when we had to go back into the empty house. The thoughts were whirling round inside my head in a confused jumble and I couldn't understand how Flora could be so cheerful.

She was actually skipping as we got off the tram and turned into our street. It was deserted except for the baker's cart half way along. The horse flicked one ear as we passed, to show that he knew we were there. Flora generally stops to pat him, but this time she ran straight past and up the front steps of our house. It was then that I realised she had made up her mind that Samuel would be there and for a moment my spirits soared as well. But although she rang the bell no one answered, and when I turned the key in the lock and pushed open the front door there was no sound except a vast, echoing silence.

"I was so sure he'd be back," Flora said in a small voice.

"I know," I nodded. "And I was sure we'd find Chang."

We looked at one another.

"I've got that awful feeling back again," Flora said after a moment.

"What sort of feeling?" I frowned.

"I can't quite describe it. Not a pain exactly, but it's here . . ." She clutched her front, somewhere between her chest and her middle. "It went for a while when we were coming home on the tram, because I was telling myself that Samuel would be here. But he isn't and now it's come back." She sank down on the bottom step of the stairs and began unlacing her boots. "It wouldn't be so bad being on our own if only we knew where he was," she went on after a moment.

"Or when he was coming back," I muttered. Flora nodded.

"I expect we could manage all right then. We did last night. It's just that deep down I'm certain that something very mysterious is going on. Something – " She stopped and stared round the hall.

"Go on," I said.

"Something dark," Flora said after a moment, almost in a whisper. "I expect you'll laugh at me, but I feel it, don't you? As though all the time we were being watched."

"That's tosh," I told her, putting the key back beside the clock so that she shouldn't see the expression on my face. "It's just one of your hunches."

"I know you despise my hunches, but this time I'm sure I'm right. I feel it here – " She thumped her middle again.

"What?" I asked. "That we're being watched?" Flora looked at me in silence for a while.

"As though someone's been here," she said. "In the house . . ." My heart had begun to pound and my mouth suddenly felt dry. Flora sat quite still with her head on one side, as though she was listening. Then she frowned. "Perhaps Samuel did come back," she said. "And now he's gone out again, looking for us."

"He wouldn't do that," I said. "Not without leaving a note."

"I'm going up to his room to see," Flora said, jumping up. "You never know."

"Hang on," I said. "I'm coming with you."

We opened the door and went in. But the room was empty and there was no sign of a portmanteau or any of Samuel's things. Everything was as tidy as it had been the day before. Flora looked round and then shook her head.

"He hasn't been here, has he?" she said.

"I knew that," I said. "If he had come back he'd have opened the letter from Nellie, but it's still sitting on the hall chair where I left it. I think you're imagining things."

"Maybe you're right," Flora said doubtfully, and then went out again.

I was just going to follow her when something caught my eye. One of the drawers of the desk was slightly open and there was a piece of paper caught in it. I frowned. Samuel is very methodical and he never leaves drawers open. What's more I was sure it hadn't been like that the day before. I could hear Flora's footsteps retreating down the stairs. I hesitated for a moment, and then went and opened the lid of the desk.

It was quite tidy inside, just as it had been when I'd taken the stamps out of the cubby hole, except that something was missing. The photograph that I had seen the day before was no longer there.

Flora was already in the kitchen when I caught up with her.

"I suppose we'll have to wash up," she said, staring glumly at the remains of our breakfast which was still sitting on the table where we'd left it.

"Leave it for a minute," I said, closing the door and standing with my back to it.

"William – what is it?" Flora asked, seeing the look on my face. I took a deep breath.

"Your hunch," I said slowly. "There must be something in it after all. Look . . . I think I ought to tell you – "

"What?" Flora asked.

"Several things, really . . ."

I sat down on the armchair and took a deep breath. Flora listened without interrupting as I told her about the desk and the photograph, and then about the Chinese man. When I'd finished she was quiet for a while.

"It wasn't a dream if that's what you're thinking," I said. "I did see him. I'm certain of that." She nodded. "And I didn't tell you before because I thought you'd be frightened."

"I expect I would have been if you'd told me last night," Flora said with a shiver. "You were too, weren't you? That's why you slept in my room. But it's all right now, in the daylight."

I could see that Flora was doing her best to be brave, but it wasn't easy, not for either of us. The sinking sensation in my stomach had come back, and even with the sun pouring into the kitchen I didn't want to think too much about the photograph, because whoever had taken it must have come into the house while we were out. I picked up the poker and began rattling it against the bars of the range. Flora watched me for a moment and then leant forward.

"I'm beginning to wonder whether Samuel's in some kind of danger," she said.

Up until that moment I had only thought about how we could find Samuel. It hadn't struck me that he might need our help, and I frowned, wondering whether Flora could be right. Of course it's hard to imagine Samuel being in any sort of danger, because he is the wisest and cleverest person I've ever known, and wherever he is he always seems to be in charge so that he inspires you with complete confidence. But so many inexplicable things were happening, and Samuel himself wasn't here to make sense of them, and supposing he did need our help. I rocked back on my heels and threw the poker into the coal bucket.

"We can't go on like this," I said. "Samuel's vanished. The doves have gone. Chang's disappeared, and now the photograph is missing. I don't think we ought to stay here on our own any longer without telling someone."

"Some other grown up, you mean?" Flora said. I nodded. "I think so, too," she agreed, suddenly looking very relieved.

It was all very well to decide we ought to tell someone. Making up our minds who it should be was much harder. The obvious person was Nellie, but we couldn't tell her unless we went back to The Cott, and anyway Nellie was worried enough about Rose. I suggested Madame Zhinovia, Flora's new ballet teacher, and Flora grew quite excited until she remembered that Madame Zhinovia had gone to Paris for a week.

"This is hopeless," Flora said. "There must be someone . . ."

"I told you we should have sent a telegram to Gus," I said. "She'd have got it by now – "

"And I said we should have talked to Fred," Flora countered, beginning to bang the heels of her boots together in a way that infuriates me whenever she does it. "He wanted to help. I know he did. And I don't believe he'd have let us be sent to the Workhouse."

We glared at one another accusingly.

"He'd have gone to the police," I said, jumping up and going over to the window. "And then – "

"The police!" Flora cut in. "William . . . maybe that's what we ought to do." I spun round and looked at her. "Well, we have had a burglary, haven't we?" she said. "Even if it is only a photograph that's missing. And the doves, of course. If Nellie was here she'd go for the police . . . I'm sure she would."

It was the most sensible idea yet, and I should have admitted it at once. But I still felt too cross, so I picked up the coal scuttle instead and stood there jiggling it by the handle.

"Why don't you say something?" Flora asked, looking aggrieved. "You know I'm right."

"No I don't," I said. "And anyway, I want to think. I'm going to fill this."

I unhooked the key to the coal shed from the nail by the back door where Nellie always hangs it, and went outside.

Our coal shed is an eerie place. It's black as ink in there and shaped like a tunnel with one small window at the end. When the coalman has just called and the coal is heaped high in front of the window you can fill the scuttle from just inside the open door, but as the pile of coal gets lower you have to go further and further into the shed, where there's only a chink of light and I always have the nasty feeling that one day someone will bang the door shut behind me and I'll be locked in.

I filled the coal scuttle as quickly as I could that day, and bolted outside into the daylight with a shudder of relief, locking the coal house door behind me. I should have been trying to decide what to say to Flora when I got back into the kitchen, but instead I looked up at the sky, which was a clear, pale blue and imagined, just for a moment, that I was in Cornwall, staying with Gus and going out fishing in the bay with Joel Tregarth. The sky is often that pale blue in Cornwall, and there were seagulls, I thought, squinting up at the white bird I could see above me, coming closer and wheeling round in an arc. It was too small for a seagull, of course. More like a pigeon. Pigeons and sparrows are the only birds you see in London. This one was coming nearer every second, diving down until I could hear the beat of its wings. And it was pure white.

I expect you've guessed by now. But I didn't. Not until the bird actually fluttered over my head and then tucked in its wings and disappeared through the opening that Samuel had made in the roof of the dovehouse. It was only then that I realised it was one of our own doves coming home.

I gave a great shout for Flora, and then, without waiting for her to appear I made for the door of the dovehouse, almost tripping

79

over the coal scuttle in my excitement. For a moment I had forgotten that the dovehouse door is always locked.

"William, what is it?" Flora asked, appearing through the kitchen door. "What's happened?"

"Come and have a look," I shouted.

By then I had fetched the stool we had been standing on the day before and was climbing on to it so that I could look through the window of the dovehouse.

"They've come back!" Flora exclaimed, running up the path. "Oh, the precious, darling things . . ."

"Not all of them," I said, trying to count.

"How many? Let me have a look." She tugged at my legs so that I nearly toppled off the stool. "Please, William . . ."

"All right," I said climbing down. "Now you count."

"Three – that's all," Flora said, screwing her head this way and that to peer through the window. "They must have escaped and flown home. So that boy was a thief . . ."

"Maybe," I said.

"What do you mean, 'maybe'. They're here, aren't they?"

"I meant maybe the boy was a thief. And maybe they've escaped." I stared thoughtfully up at the sky. "Or maybe they were released . . ." Flora turned round and looked at me. Then her eyes widened and she jumped off the stool.

"By Samuel! Is that what you're thinking?"

"It's funny that only three have come back," I said, squinting up at the sky again. "That's why I think they must have been released."

"And who else but Samuel would know that they'd fly home?" Flora said. "It must have been him. And if it was that means he'll be back soon to make sure they've arrived safely."

Suddenly things didn't seem quite so bad. It was as though the doves themselves had brought a beam of hope.

"Perhaps we shan't have to go to the police after all," I said.

Of course we both expected that Samuel would turn up quite soon after that, and even when the minutes ticked past and there was no sound of his key in the lock we still didn't give up hope.

"We'll give him until two o'clock," I said.

"That's a whole hour," Flora said, looking at the clock. "I'm sure he'll be back long before then."

But it wasn't Samuel who came.

We were sitting at the range eating bread and dripping when it happened. Flora and I weren't talking much because both of us were straining our ears for the sound of footsteps coming up the front steps, so it was quiet in the kitchen except for the coals stirring in the range and the distant cry of an oyster seller in Kennington Road. And then, from quite close by, we heard someone whistling. Flora lifted her head and looked at me, but Samuel always whistles Pop Goes the Weasel. This sounded more like Cockles and Mussels Alive, Alive'Oh. It was coming from somewhere behind the house. Then the whistling stopped, and almost at once we heard another sound.

Flora was half way towards the window when I grabbed her.

"That's not Samuel," I whispered, pulling her down on to the floor. We crawled the rest of the way on all fours and peered over the window sill.

The gate was wide open and through the archway came a boy. He must have been about the same age as me, and he was wearing a cloth cap that came right down over his ears and almost met the muffler that was wound round his neck, and a huge white apron. He had propped his barrow in the archway to hold the gate open, and on it we could see a couple of oyster barrels. Without a moment's hesitation he came quickly down the garden path. Flora and I both ducked our heads out of sight and I felt her clutch my arm convulsively

"That's him," she whispered. "That's the boy I saw last night. What shall we do?"

"Ssh," I whispered, keeping a tight hold on her arm. I guessed that Flora was all for dashing out there, but I wasn't sure whether the boy had come alone, and I wanted to see what he would do. I raised my head slightly above the window sill again. He must have unlocked the door to the dovehouse, because it was open, and almost before I had time to duck again I saw him come out, tucking something wrapped in a cloth inside the front of his apron. He locked the door behind him and hurried back up the garden path. When he reached the barrow he whipped the cloth off the top of one of the oyster barrels and laid the bundle gently down inside, tucking the cloth around it again. The next moment he had turned the barrow round and was going out through the gate again and we heard him locking it behind him.

The whole thing had happened so fast that there hadn't been time to decide what to do. But I was on my feet now and pulling Flora up after me.

"He's taken the doves away again, hasn't he?" she gasped. "They were in that bundle – and now it's too late."

"No it isn't," I said. "We're going after him . . ."

"Follow him, you mean?" I nodded.

"He must be taking them to Samuel, and this is our best chance of finding him." Flora stared at me for a second, but there was no time to be lost. Already the sound of whistling was growing fainter. "Quick," I told her. "Run out to the front and see which way he goes when he turns out of the alleyway – and don't let him see you."

"My boots!" Flora exclaimed, starting to bend down and lace them up. "And my coat – "

"There's no time for that now," I told her. "You can do it when you get to the corner. And I'll bring your coat . . . only run!" I pushed her towards the kitchen door.

As soon as she'd gone I raced out to the back. One look was enough. The doves had definitely gone. I bolted the back door after me and ran upstairs two at a time, grabbing Flora's coat from the hook as I passed.

When I reached the street I could see her waving to me from the corner.

"That way," she shouted. "Towards Kennington Road." We began to run.

"I'm sure we'll never catch up with him," Flora panted, as we raced round the corner, narrowly missing a woman with a shopping basket.

"We don't want to catch him," I told her. "Just to see where he's going."

In spite of having to trundle his barrow the boy must have been going quite fast, because he was already some way ahead of us, half way along Kennington Road. I was afraid that he'd give us the slip when he reached the cross roads at the bottom. There are four roads leading from it and he might go down any one of them, so I began to run faster to narrow the distance between us.

"William – I can't . . ." Flora called. "My boot – it's half off . . ."

Over my shoulder I could see that she had stopped to lace it up again. The boy had reached the corner by then and I slowed down a bit as he looked left and right and waited to let a hansom go past, and at that moment he turned round and stared back down the street towards me. I stopped and leant against the railings, trying to look as if I was just waiting for Flora who was still running to catch up with me and was crimson by then from having bent double to tie her laces.

"You might have waited," she gasped, stopping beside me. "We wouldn't have lost him . . . he's still there."

"He didn't see you, did he?" I frowned. "When you were on the corner? Because he looked straight at me just now." Flora shook her head.

"No, I'm sure he didn't," she said. "Anyway, he's not looking now. He's talking to someone." An elderly gentleman had come up to the barrow and seemed to be asking if he could buy a dozen oysters, and we could see the boy shaking his head and pointing to the barrels as though he was saying they had all gone. The old gentleman turned away and began to walk towards us, and the next moment the boy had dived across the road.

"Come on," I said, beginning to run again.

"You don't think he's guessed that we're following him, do you?" Flora asked anxiously, as we sped past the elderly gentleman. "Suppose he stops and asks us what we want."

"He's in too much of a hurry to do that," I said. "Look!" We had reached the corner by then, and across the street where the road divides I caught sight of the boy moving quickly away from us in the direction of the river. For a moment he was lost to view as a tram rattled past, and then we saw him again, trundling the barrow as fast as he could along the street.

"He's going towards Blackfriar's Bridge," I said as soon as we were safely over the road. The boy was still quite a long way ahead of us, trotting doggedly on close to the kerb so that the hansom cabs and four wheelers had to pull out to pass him. He was going faster than ever, I thought, but he didn't turn round or slow down even when a woman called to him from the steps of her house and pointed to the oyster barrels. Ahead of us we could see the piers of Blackfriar's Bridge.

"William, he's going to cross it," Flora gasped, slowing down to catch her breath and looking at me despairingly. "You know I'm not sure that this was a good idea after all," she went on, stopping altogether and leaning against someone's front gate.

"Come on," I told her. She shook her head.

"I can't, not for a minute. I've got a stitch, and it's such a long way. Besides, we don't know where he's going." I glanced over my shoulder. The boy was some way ahead of us and still moving.

"Touch your toes," I told her. "We can't give up now. Just keep thinking that we'll be with Samuel soon. That's what I'm doing."

After a moment Flora straightened up, looking rather pink.

"It's gone now," she said. "Do you really think we're going to find him?"

"We must," I said grimly. "And if we don't we'll take a hansom back home and go to the police. Can you run again now?"

"I'll try," she nodded.

Fog was beginning to creep up from the river as we crossed the bridge, misting the brown sails of the barges and wherries on the water below us. Ahead we could see the dome of St Paul's Cathedral, with all the other spiky spires and weathervanes of the city's churches around it, rising up through the fog. We were coming to a part of London that neither of us knew, and I felt half excited and half afraid as we followed the boy off the bridge and up into the narrow, twisting cobbled streets that led towards the top of Ludgate Hill.

Of course we still didn't have the least idea where the boy was going, or who he was, or where we should find ourselves when we reached the end of our journey. But none of that seemed to matter any longer, because it was all rather like a dream by then. Somehow we had to keep going on, I thought, and in the end we would find Samuel and he would explain it all.

I glanced at Flora. She hadn't complained once, or even lagged behind since we reached the bridge, and her eyes were fixed ahead, as though she dared not stop staring at the boy's back even for a second. Her face was set in a kind of look she wears when she's doing her ballet exercises.

"It can't be much further," I said, and at that moment a great bell began to boom through the fog just ahead of us. All around it the other church clocks chimed in, striking three and we saw the boy put on a sudden spurt as though they had reminded him that he was late. Then he turned a corner and was gone. I began to run, suddenly afraid that at the last minute we would lose him amongst the narrow streets.

"Which way did he go?" Flora gasped, catching up with me as I rounded the corner and stopped.

All at once we had left the twisting, cobbled lanes behind us and I saw that we had come out on the top of Ludgate Hill. Ahead of us St Paul's Cathedral loomed up through the mist and everywhere there were people coming and going. Carriages rattled up and down the hill, and above the tread of feet and the jingle of shop bells was the clatter of horses' hooves, the shouts of the drivers and somewhere quite close by a man selling evening newspapers. But the boy had vanished into the crowd.

"Which way?" Flora asked again.

"I don't know," I said, feeling empty inside. "We've lost him."

"We can't have done," Flora said. "He must be here somewhere . . ." She looked wildly round.

"It's no use," I said, shaking my head miserably. "We'll never find him now. Anyway, I can't think what Samuel would be doing here. We must have made a mistake." Flora put her hand on my arm.

"Please," she said. "We've come all this way . . . we can't give up now. Let's go on looking, just for a while. If we can't find him, then we'll have to go to the police."

It had been my idea to follow the boy in the first place, so after a moment I nodded even though I felt sure it was hopeless.

"Which way?" I said. "I didn't even see if he turned left or right?"

"This way," Flora said, pointing up the hill. I followed her, but as we threaded our way along the street, peering down every alley and into every courtyard our search began to seem more and more like a wild goose chase.

"He's probably in Shoreditch or Bethnal Green by now," I muttered at last.

"I'm going to try the other way," Flora said obstinately as we retraced our steps down the hill. The fog was thicker than ever. I

86

could feel it creeping down inside my collar and around my neck. We had just passed the lane we turned out of when Flora gave a sudden squeal.

"Look!" She cried, pointing under an arch into a small, paved courtyard.

On one side there were houses with black iron railings and steps leading up to them. On the other side was a bookseller. By the light of the street lamp that swung from the arch we could see that the shop was dingy, with peeling brown paint on the door and the shutters. There was a tray of books outside, and next to it stood the cart with the oyster barrels on it.

CHAPTER EIGHT

In which we meet the Bookseller of Paternoster Court . . .

"I told you he wasn't far away, didn't I?" Flora said, giving me a triumphant look. "And I was right. I just knew we'd find him." She started to walk off under the archway.

"Where are you going?" I said, catching hold of her arm.

"Into the shop, of course," Flora said. "That's where the boy's gone, so Samuel must be there as well."

It didn't seem very likely, I thought, looking at the peeling paint and the dusty rows of books beyond the yellowish glass. Even though it had been my idea to follow the boy I'd never expected that we'd end up somewhere like this. I wasn't sure that I wanted to go into the shop, not at once anyway, and I certainly didn't want Flora to go in there without me.

"Oh do come on, William," she said, trying to wriggle out of my grasp.

"Wait a minute," I said. "This doesn't make sense, does it? I mean . . . what would Samuel be doing in there?"

"Nothing makes sense," Flora said quickly. "Samuel disappearing or Chang or the doves . . . or anything. But at least we've found the cart. The boy must have gone into that shop. And if Samuel's not there, well someone will know where he is – "

"Unless the boy's a thief after all," I cut in. Flora shook her head.

"I'm sure he isn't," she said. "In fact, I'm quite certain about it now." She looked towards the shop.

"I suppose this is another of your hunches," I frowned.

"It's more than a hunch," she said, in quite a definite way. For a moment I stared at her.

"There's something you haven't told me. Isn't there?" Flora nodded. "Well go on then," I said, letting go of her arm.

"It was this morning," she said, "before you woke up. I was looking round – not for anything really, just sort of looking and wishing that Samuel was there. I went into his room first, and then I went into the spare room, the one that Chang was in . . ." She stopped.

"Go on," I told her.

"There was a book on the table, so I had a look at it, to see if there were any pictures, you know. It was quite dull actually . . . Travels on the North West Frontier or something . . . anyway as I was looking through it a piece of paper fell out . . . like a curl paper. It said 'Parrish and Partridge – Booksellers, Paternoster Court, St Paul's Churchyard . . .'" She stopped and looked at me. "Don't you see, William? That's what this shop is called. Look!"

I stared under the archway at the shop front.

"Why didn't you tell me before?" I asked.

"I forgot, I suppose," Flora said. "It didn't seem important. Then, when we were coming over the bridge and I could see St Paul's, I remembered again and I just wondered . . . that was why I wouldn't give up, you see. Not till we'd found the shop."

All at once it seemed as though Samuel really might be close by, and a wave of excitement shot through me.

"Come on," I said.

Flora was close behind me as I pushed the door open and went inside. The shop was dimly lit by two flickering oil lamps which hung from the ceiling, and there was a strong smell of lamp oil and old, damp books. The books were everywhere, piled up on trestle tables and on the counter and lining the shelves, row after row of them. They were even stacked in heaps on the floor.

Beyond the bookshelves, at the very back of the shop, a light was shining around the cracks of a closed door. But there didn't seem to be anyone in the shop, and as the jangling of the bell faded away an eerie silence fell.

The stillness seemed to wrap damp fingers around us, and for two pins I would have turned round and run outside again. We stood there, peering into the shadows, but neither of us said a word. Then I heard Flora give a gasp.

"Look!" She whispered, pointing towards the back of the shop.

Down at the far end of the high counter a ghostly face had suddenly appeared from behind a pile of books, and was staring at us. At first all I could make out was a pale blob and two huge, unblinking eyes. My heart had begun to thump so that I had to force myself to take a step closer, and as I did so I saw that the face belonged to a little girl. She was quite ordinary looking, too, and not at all ghost-like now that I could see her more clearly, even though she was so thin and pale. She didn't move as I came up to the counter with Flora close on my heels. It was Flora who broke the silence.

"You gave us quite a fright," she said crossly. "Why didn't you say something?"

"Don't know," the girl whispered, flicking a quick look over her shoulder towards the lighted doorway.

"Well if I was minding the shop I'd ask people what they wanted," Flora went on, relief making her bossy, "not hide behind a pile of books like that. You were hiding, weren't you?"

"Don't know nothing about no books," the girl said, shrinking back.

"Never mind about the books," I said, frowning at Flora. "We don't want to buy one anyway. We're looking for someone, that's all, and we think he came in here. A boy – "

"An oyster seller," Flora cut in. "That's his barrow outside . . . he is here, isn't he?" The girl looked from one to the other of us and then began twisting her hair round her fingers.

"Look," I said, "is anyone here? Anyone at all? We're really looking for our Guardian. He's tall and . . ." I stopped. It wasn't going to be easy to describe Samuel, and the girl was looking more wary than ever. I had a sudden feeling that she was waiting for something to happen.

"He generally wears a big black hat," Flora cut in, "and his name is Samuel Rolandson . . ."

A sort of twitch passed over the girl's face at the sound of Samuel's name and she scrambled off the stool she had been perched on and began to back away from us towards the lighted doorway.

"Where are you going?" I said. She stopped for a moment and stared at us. "Just tell us if you've seen him . . . or the boy . . ."

"You're to stop 'ere," she gabbled suddenly. "You're not to come no closer, mind."

"All right, all right," I said. "But just tell us where you're going."

"Ter fetch 'im," she said. Flora and I looked at one another.

"Samuel, you mean?" Flora said. But the girl shook her head.

"No, not 'im. . . . *'Im* – wot 'as the shop. I don't know nothing about none of this, see. So you just wait – will yer?"

Somewhere in the distance, beyond the lighted doorway, I thought I heard a door close. I frowned.

"Can't we come with you?" I said. "Then we could tell him ourselves – "

"And it would save time," Flora nodded. The little girl shot a quick look over her shoulder, and then backed towards the door, shaking her head violently.

"But why not?" I said. "Look, this is important . . . we have to find Samuel."

"You've seen him, haven't you?" Flora cut in. "And that boy – the oyster seller . . . you know about him too – "

"I don't know nothing," the girl said, shaking her head more violently than ever and backing against the door with a thump. By now she was looking really frightened. Then, from inside the room we heard the sound of footsteps approaching. The handle was turned and the door swung open. Someone stood, framed in the doorway.

The room beyond was brightly lit and it was hard at first to make out more than an outline, so that just for a moment I thought it might be Samuel. I took a quick step forward and then stopped. It was a man, but he wasn't as tall as Samuel, and he was old, too, and rather stooped, and I saw that he wore gold spectacles and had a great deal of mutton chop whiskers and beard around his face.

"Crumpets," he said, almost to himself, as though he'd been trying to make up his mind for some time and had finally decided. "Where is that child? Emily ... ah yes, good, there you are. Crumpets. Six of the best from the shop on the corner. And half a pound of butter ..."

"'Scuse me," said the little girl.

"Can't have crumpets without butter," the old man said, paying no attention. "Can we?"

"'Scuse me, if you please – " she said, a bit louder this time, catching hold of his sleeve and jerking her head in our direction.

"And black currant jam ... well? What is it?"

"Someone ter see yer – that's wot," she said, twisting her head round and staring at us.

"Someone to see me? A customer? Well, why didn't you say so before? About the Dickens first edition, is it?" He began to peer vaguely from side to side.

"They ain't no customers," the little girl said, lowering her voice to a whisper. "They come about – "

"Not customers, eh? Dear me – well where are they, then?"

"We're here," Flora said, suddenly pushing past me and marching right up to the old gentleman.

"Ah yes, that's better. I can see you now. Two of you, is it? A girl and a boy. I don't suppose you'd be interested in the Dickens, would you?" He gazed mildly at me over Flora's shoulder.

"I'm afraid not," I said. "We're looking for someone – "

"That boy who came into the shop not so long ago," Flora cut in. "The one who left his barrow outside."

"Pity," the old gentleman said vaguely. "Time was when I could have sold that edition within a week. But nowadays . . . ah well." He sighed. "A boy, you say?"

"Yes," I said. "We're quite sure that he came in here."

"And he had some doves with him," Flora nodded.

"Doves? Indeed . . . let me think now – what was I . . . ?" He broke off and looked first at Flora and then at me and stroked his beard as though he was doing his best to remember. I noticed then that he was wearing gloves. They were grey with pearl buttons, and I was wondering whether he'd just come in and had forgotten to take them off, because no one wears gloves indoors, when he stopped stroking his beard.

"Crumpets!" He exclaimed, his gaze coming to rest on the girl who was still leaning against the door and staring at us with her mouth open. "That's it! Crumpets. It must have been the Dickens that drove them out of my head."

The girl straightened up and looked at him, and I shot a despairing glance at Flora.

"Six of the best now, Emily," he went on, putting his hand into his pocket. "Half a pound of butter and a pot of blackcurrant jam. That will be most suitable, I think – and here's half a crown. Can you remember all that?" The girl shifted from one foot to the other and nodded, but she didn't move from the doorway. "I want you to be as quick as you can," the old gentleman said, peering down at her. "And come straight back." I saw her nod again, but she still didn't move. "Well? What are you waiting for then?"

She gave him a funny, quick look and opened her mouth to say something, but before any words could come out he had put his hand on her shoulder and was hurrying her past us towards the door.

"After that you can run along home," we heard him say. "It won't do to keep you out after dark, eh? The fog's coming down – "

The shop door jangled and as they stood in the doorway I saw him bend down to say something to her. Beyond them the fog had settled in a soft, yellow blanket over the courtyard, so that even the houses opposite were hidden, and although I screwed up my eyes I couldn't make out whether the cart was still there or not.

All at once the shadowy shop with its piles of musty smelling books seemed an uneasy, fearful place, and I spun round, meaning to tell Flora that we ought not to wait any longer, but just make a dash for it before the old bookseller came back. Samuel wasn't here. I was certain of that now and I felt heavy with foreboding.

It was too late, though. Flora had ducked past me without a word and was standing in the back room, gazing curiously around her. Before I could move I heard the shop door close, and with surprising suddenness the old gentleman was beside me again and peering thoughtfully into my face.

"Now let me see – where were we?" he murmured. "The Dickens, wasn't it? A very fine first edition – a little foxing here and there in some of the volumes, but otherwise in excellent condition." He paused, looking about him for a moment. "I'm sorry your friend couldn't wait," he went on, "but if you like I could show you. I have it in the back."

"She's not my friend," I began, looking towards the back room where Flora was quite clearly visible, standing in the middle of a blue and red Turkey carpet with her hands behind her back.

"Indeed?" he said mildly, resting his hand on my elbow and

steering me towards the doorway. "Do forgive me. I was under the impression you were together."

"We are," I said.

"You are? Dear me, this is most confusing."

"What William means," Flora said, beginning to explain, "is that we're not friends . . . well, not just friends. He's my brother."

"Your brother? Ah yes, now I understand. And you found your way in here all right, I see." He had let go of my elbow and was looking quite intently at Flora, so that she began to wriggle uncomfortably.

"It didn't say 'private' – and the door was wide open," she said.

"No doubt you were looking for the Dickens," he nodded, pottering over to a large, dusty table which was piled high with books and beginning to search through them. "Now where did I put it?"

"We don't want to buy anything," I said, beginning to feel desperate. I shot a quick look at Flora and then walked over to the table and, putting both my hands on the top of one of the piles of books, I leant across to him. "We don't want the Dickens first edition, or whatever it is. We only came in here because we're looking for someone. We told you – "

"Not want it?" He drew back, looking puzzled.

"A boy," Flora cut in. "The boy we asked you about . . . did he come in here or not?"

"We don't mean to be rude," I said, "but we have to find him."

"A boy, you say?" He looked from one to the other of us in bewilderment. Then, just as I'd made up my mind that he was quite mad he seemed to remember. "Ah yes," he murmured. "You told me, didn't you? So it's not the Dickens after all."

"No," we said in unison.

"And this boy you're looking for – what's his name?"

"We don't know his name," Flora said, her voice beginning to rise. "All we know is that he must have come in here because his barrow was outside – "

"And he must have brought some doves in with him," I cut in.

"Doves . . . ah yes. But you don't know his name, you say?"

"The doves don't belong to him," I frowned. "They belong to Samuel Rolandson – "

"He's our Guardian," Flora interrupted. "And it's him we're really looking for. We haven't seen him since Friday morning, and we don't know where he's gone." All at once the old gentleman was really listening, and in her haste to tell him everything Flora's words tumbled over each other. "That boy, the one we're trying to find, he came and took the doves away and we followed him here because we thought he must be taking them to Samuel. But it hasn't turned out right, because Samuel isn't here after all, and if you can't tell us where to find him I don't know what we're going to do . . . except go to the police . . ." She stopped with a gulp, and then, suddenly overwhelmed by it all, she burst into tears.

"Dear me," the old gentleman murmured. "Dear me, this seems to be more serious than I had thought."

"It's worse than serious," I said angrily, putting my arm round Flora and wishing that she'd stop crying. "It's about the worst thing that's ever happened to us, and we've walked all the way here, and waited and waited because we were so sure that the boy must have come into the shop – "

"Yes, yes, I see . . .'

"But you haven't told us anything," I went on.

"And we have to find Samuel," Flora sobbed, shaking me off as fresh tears ran down her cheeks. "We have to – "

"Dear me," the old gentleman exclaimed, looking agitated himself, and then producing a very clean white handkerchief from his pocket, which he shook out and handed to Flora. "Dear me, yes I see. And you came here quite alone? There was no one with you?" He looked at me while Flora wiped her eyes and blew her nose.

"Of course we came alone," I frowned.

"Without your poor mother . . . she sent you, I suppose."

Flora's sobs had just begun to die down, but now she began crying harder than ever. Generally we don't mind telling people that we're orphans, but that afternoon, not knowing where Samuel was or what we were going to do next, it seemed the last straw.

"We haven't got a mother," I muttered, staring down at the blue and red Turkey carpet and feeling like crying myself. "Samuel adopted us when we were babies."

"And he looks after you – all alone?"

"No," I said. "There's Nellie. But her sister's ill at the moment and she had to stay down in the country with her. That's why we came back to London on our own, you see . . ."

Something made me stop then and look up, and as I did so it seemed to me that the old bookseller had changed. He was no longer stooping to peer at us through his gold rimmed spectacles, but standing very still and straight, so that he looked taller. His vague, bewildered expression had gone, too, and I saw that he was listening very intently as he smoothed one of the leather bound books in front of him with his grey gloved fingers.

I suppose that it was only a second before he raised his head, but I knew by then that something was wrong. The bookseller was somehow not what he seemed, and I was afraid that we had made a horrible mistake.

"Not serious, I trust," he said gently, pushing the book to one side as our eyes met, and stooping towards me a little so that he looked old again. "The illness . . ."

I glanced at Flora and swallowed. She was still sobbing into the handkerchief and hadn't noticed anything. I wanted to warn her, but he was still watching me.

"Pneumonia," I muttered.

"Dear me . . . And you say that you haven't seen your Guardian, Samuel . . . Samuel Rolandson, isn't it – since Friday?"

"Saturday," Flora gulped, rolling the handkerchief into a ball between her hands. "Chang arrived on Friday, didn't he, William? And that's how it all began. All this is his fault . . . everything was perfectly ordinary until he came."

The bookseller was nodding and looking intently at her, and I shot a quick look round. My mind was racing and I had suddenly remembered the sound I'd heard when we were talking to Emily; the sound of a door closing in the distance. But there was no door. I could see a window with green velvet curtains drawn across it, but otherwise the room was as full of books as the shop itself. They lined each wall and stood in piles on the floor and the table in front of us, and the only door leading from the room was the one we had come through.

"Chang," the bookseller murmured, running his hand over the pile of books again and then picking one up and setting it down carefully with the spine towards us. "Chang . . . I seem to recall that name." We could have gone then and there, and I was about to nudge Flora when he looked up again. "Chinese, I presume."

"Yes, he's a magician, like Samuel," Flora nodded.

"And an old friend of Mr Rolandson's perhaps," he said, looking at me as he spoke.

"I believe you know Samuel after all," Flora said, staring at him. "Don't you?"

"I have had the privilege of supplying your Guardian with certain volumes from time to time," he nodded. "The last occasion was – ah . . . now let me think . . . when would it be? Quite recently, I'm certain of that. But precisely when . . ." His voice trailed away, and I could see that Flora was holding her breath expectantly as she stared at him.

"Was it today?" she asked, taking a step forward. "Do please try to remember – "

"Today?" He looked at her vaguely."Today? I believe not. And now he's vanished. Dear me, what a coil! A conundrum, one might almost say." He shook his head. "What can be done?" Flora opened her mouth but before she could say anything his face had suddenly brightened, and he gave a quick nod. "Crumpets," he declared. "That's the answer. Crumpets! Yes indeed . . . now where can that child have got to? I told her to come straight back . . . yes, we will sit by the fire and have crumpets and blackcurrant jam and talk the whole thing over – "

"We don't want any crumpets," I said, seizing Flora's arm and trying to drag her towards the door. "I'm afraid we can't wait any longer. We have to go now."

"But William – " Flora began, obstinately refusing to move.

"Come on," I told her. "It's getting late."

The old gentleman wasn't listening, though. He was already half way to the door and murmuring to himself.

"Foolish child . . . I must find out where she is . . . not lost in the fog, I hope. Dear me, dear me . . ." By this time he had one grey gloved hand on the door knob and he seemed to have forgotten about us.

"I think William's right," Flora said, looking at him doubtfully as I gave her another push. "Perhaps we ought to be going."

"No, no . . . indeed not," he replied, turning quite suddenly to look at us both as he opened the door. "You shall stay here and keep warm beside the fire until I come back with the crumpets. Patience . . . yes, that's the word. Patience. I am convinced that we will find the solution to all this if you will wait just a little longer."

"I'm sorry, we can't wait," I said, pulling Flora after me.

But it was too late.

"Patience," he said softly, whisking round the door as we got there.

Then he banged it shut and we heard the key turn in the lock.

CHAPTER NINE

In which we jump out of the frying pan into the fire, and discover a friend . . .

"He's locked us in," Flora exclaimed, staring at the door in disbelief as the old gentleman's footsteps shuffled away into the distance.

"It's no use," I told her, watching as she beat her hand against the door and twisted the handle this way and that. Then the shop bell jangled, and with an ominous thump that door was slammed shut, too.

Flora leant against the locked door and looked at me.

"He was pretending all the time," she said. "I don't believe he's gone to find the girl at all, do you?"

"No." I shook my head. "It was just an excuse – like the crumpets. I tried to warn you."

"I know," she nodded. "Only I didn't realise until it was too late."

"It was all pretence," I said angrily. "All that twaddle about crumpets and blackcurrant jam and first editions . . . I don't believe he's a real bookseller at all. He just wanted to keep us here until he'd found out everything we knew. And he didn't tell us a single thing." I stared at the locked door and then shoved my hands deep into my pockets wondering how we could have been so stupid.

Flora slid slowly to the ground and sat with her back against one of the piles of books. After a moment she gave a kind of shudder and buried her face in her hands.

"You're not going to start crying again, are you?" I said, watching her. "Because we've got to think."

"I don't believe I can cry any more," she said, lifting her head and looking up at me solemnly. "It's too bad for that now."

"About as bad as it can be," I muttered.

"I'm afraid that Samuel really must be in some kind of dreadful danger," she said after a moment. "I think that horrid old man knows all about it, too. But he wouldn't tell us, and now he's locked us in so we can't even go to the police."

"And the worst part is that no one knows we're here," I nodded.

"He could keep us locked up for days," Flora looked fearfully round the room.

"It wouldn't be quite so bad if only we knew what was happening," I frowned. "But everything's such an awful jumble."

"Like an impossible jig saw puzzle," Flora said.

"Chang must have something to do with it," I said, beginning to walk up and down the room and ticking things off on my fingers in the way that Samuel does when he's trying to make sense out of a problem. "Only we don't know what. And the boy – he's part of it as well – "

"And the old man," Flora cut in. "Because of the book I saw in the spare room. . . . and he did admit in the end that he knows Samuel."

"But he didn't tell us anything about the boy," I said. "So we still don't know if it was Samuel who sent him to collect the doves."

"We don't even know if the boy really brought them in here," Flora said gloomily. "I mean – where are they?" She looked round the room.

I had walked round to the far side of the table by then, and was standing where the old gentleman had stood, looking down at the books that were piled up there all higgledy piggledy. There was a space on that side of the table, as though everything had been pushed to one side. And it was then that I saw it, resting against the bottom of a stack of books.

"Look at this," I exclaimed, giving a low whistle.

"What is it?" Flora asked. I picked it up carefully and held it between my finger and thumb so that she could see. "A feather!" She scrambled to her feet. "One of the doves' feathers." I nodded. "So he was in here." She touched it gently with her finger.

"He must have been in this room when we first came into the shop," I said. "And don't you remember? While we were out there, talking to the girl, a door closed somewhere. I heard it . . . I know I did . . ."

For a moment we looked at one another.

"But there isn't another door," Flora frowned, staring round the room.

"I know that," I said. "But by the time the old man opened this door, the boy had gone. So how did he get out?"

"A secret door – " Flora's eyes widened.

"He must have got out somehow," I said. "There's one door and one window – "

"The window!"

But when Flora pulled back the curtains we could see that it was set with heavy iron bars, about two inches apart, and it didn't look as though it had been opened for years because it was thick with grime and cobwebs.

"There must be another way out," I said, shaking my head. "And we've got to find it."

Of course we'd both read stories about secret sliding panels leading into priest's holes where people could hide, but this room didn't have any panelling. I had an idea that there might be a doorway disguised by shelves of books, so while Flora held the lamp high I examined every shelf to see whether there was a crack which would show us a doorway. We worked our way right round the room, stopping from time to time to listen, just in case the old gentleman came creeping back and surprised us, but there was no sound from beyond the locked door, and by the time we arrived back where we had started from we hadn't found anything.

"I don't believe there can be a way out after all," Flora said despondently. She had sat down on the floor again and was pulling at the fringe on the blue and red Turkey carpet.

"If it had been an obvious sort of door he wouldn't just have locked us in and left us," I frowned. "He must have been pretty certain that we wouldn't find it."

It isn't a very comfortable feeling, knowing that you're someone's prisoner and wondering what's going to happen next, especially when you can't see any possible way of escaping. All sorts of horrible imaginings were rushing through my mind at that moment, and to stop myself thinking I walked all round the room once more and then went over to the window and shook the bars, just to make certain. But they were solidly fixed to the frame, and even if we had been able to rip them away I could see that the walls of the courtyard outside were too high for us to climb over. It was quite dark by then, and the fog seemed to be thicker than ever. All the shops must be shutting, I thought, and people would be hurrying home for tea. There was no clock in the room, but just then the bell on St Paul's began to strike with a deep, booming sound.

"Five o'clock," I said, when the last stroke had died away. "We've been here for almost two hours."

"I don't believe he's going to come back at all," Flora said in a small voice. "I think he's going to leave us here to starve to death."

"What tosh!" I muttered. I was beginning to feel very frightened all the same.

"I suppose that's why he told us we'd have to be patient," she said, running her hand along the pattern on the carpet. I watched her, not knowing what to say. It had grown very still. "Do you know," she went on after a moment, "when I do this I can feel a sort of bumpy line underneath. It goes almost to the edge, and then it stops."

"I suppose it's one of the floorboards," I shrugged.

"I don't think so," Flora said, shaking her head. "It's too – " She reached out her arm and began to feel under the carpet, and suddenly she gave a cry of excitement. "William – quick! Come and look . . . I think I've found it." As she spoke she scrambled off the carpet and together we rolled it back until we could see the line.

"A trap door," I said. "Of course . . ."

"Where do you suppose it leads?" she asked.

"I don't know," I said, "but this must be the way the boy went."

I took hold of the iron ring that was let into one end of the trap door and began to heave. As soon as I'd raised it an inch or so and Flora could get her fingers under the edge she helped me, and together we managed to pull it open and lower it back against the carpet.

A flight of wooden steps led down into what must have been a cellar below the shop. It was pitch dark, and a gust of cold, damp air came up to greet us, but somewhere down there I guessed that there must be a door leading to the area. All we had to do was find it and trust to luck that it wasn't locked from the outside.

"Fetch the lamp," I told Flora. "When I get half way down you can hand it to me." She nodded, and a moment later she was back.

"What can you see?" she asked, as I held it up. "There aren't any rats down there?"

"You'd better come down," I said. "And hurry . . ."

It was quite a large cellar, stacked with wooden crates that might have had books in them. At the far end I could make out a small window, and not far from it there was a door.

My heart was pounding as I waited for Flora to climb down the ladder. It took her ages, because she got her skirt caught on a nail and had to pull it free, and I knew that at any moment the old gentleman might come back and notice the light from the lamp through the area window.

"That's the second skirt I've torn in two days," she said, inspecting the damage. "Nellie will be furious with me – "

"Never mind about your skirt," I muttered, grabbing her wrist. "Just keep your fingers crossed that the door's not locked from the outside."

"What will we do if it is?" Flora said as we squeezed past the crates.

"Break the window, I suppose," I told her grimly. "We have to get out of here before he comes back. And when we do – "

"We're going to the police," Flora nodded. We looked at one another for a moment in the leaping shadows made by the lamp. Then I slid back the bolts on the door, took a deep breath and turned the handle.

"It's all right," I grinned. "It's open. You stay here while I make sure the coast is clear."

Outside the fog was so thick that I could only just make out the houses on the opposite side of the courtyard, and the street lamp at the far end was no more than a dim glow through the yellow haze. I could feel it clammy on my face and hands as I crept across the area and stood, gripping the railings and listening. But there was no sound. The courtyard seemed to be deserted.

"There's no one here," I whispered to Flora, who was still standing just inside the doorway, holding the lamp. "Quick!" The next moment she had blown it out and was beside me.

The iron gate at the top of the area steps gave a creak as I pushed it open. Then we were in the courtyard and making for the archway.

The fog seemed to hang there more thickly than ever and we had to feel our way along with one hand on the wall. Once I thought I heard the sound of footsteps nearby, only I couldn't tell whether they were in front or behind, and when I stopped for a moment to listen there was no sound. Then I saw the glow of the street lamps piercing the fog just ahead of us, and the next instant we were through the archway and out on the pavement.

"We've done it!" Flora exclaimed with a gasp of relief. "We're free! Hurry, William – we must get further away."

"But which way?" I hesitated. I didn't know any police station nearby and the fog was so thick that I was afraid we would get lost. All the shops were closed and there was no one about.

Suddenly, like a miracle, or so it seemed at the time, we heard the sound of hooves and saw the shape of a hansom looming through the fog and coming slowly along the street towards us. The driver must have been waiting, hoping to pick up a fare, I thought, and hearing our voices had moved his horse towards us. If ever there was a moment to take a hansom this was it, and I stepped forward.

"Are you free?" I called out. The driver reined in his horse and stopped just beside us.

"Only waiting for you," he said, his voice muffled by the fog. "Hop in." Instead of getting down from the box to help us he gave a low whistle which I supposed was a signal to his horse to stand still.

"Do you know where the nearest police station is?" I asked, opening the door of the cab.

"So that's where you want to go, is it?" he replied.

Flora usually leaps into a hansom as soon as the door is open, and she had one foot on the step already, but something about the driver's voice made her stop and look at me uneasily.

"I'm not sure if I like him very much," she whispered. I peered up and down the street, but there wasn't another hansom to be seen.

"We must get away from here," I muttered.

"Yes, you're right," she nodded, getting in. I followed her, but before I could close the door I heard the cab driver's voice.

"Room for one more," he said harshly.

And then there was a figure slipping out of the fog and coming towards us. With horrible swiftness he vaulted into the cab, and I saw a bobbing pigtail and narrow eyes that glittered as he slammed the door shut and turned towards us. Instantly the cab jolted forward; I heard Flora give a scream and reached desperately for the door on the far side.

"No speaky, no screamy," he said. "You go sleepy now."

He had pulled out a bottle and was turning it upside down on to a piece of material, and then with one quick movement he had seized Flora and was pressing the stuff against her face.

"Stop that!" I shouted. "Leave my sister alone . . ." I saw her struggle for a moment as I tried to reach her, and then suddenly go limp and fall in a huddle on the seat. The Chinese man nodded, hissing softly through his teeth, and coming closer to me as I backed away, kicking and yelling. The next instant he had twisted my arm behind my back and I could smell something sweet and sickly, and the last thing I remember was the sound of wheels grinding on the cobbles and the laughter of the cab driver as we careered on through the fog.

It was dark and cold when I opened my eyes. My head was throbbing and I felt sick. At first I thought that I must have fallen out of bed and be lying on the oil cloth. I closed my eyes again and lay still, hoping the pain would stop and half expecting to hear Nellie riddling out the range downstairs. But instead there was a creaking, groaning sound. And why, I wondered, did the floor keep moving? If only it would stop then perhaps I shouldn't feel so sick. I opened my eyes again, still trying to make it out. This time I could see a faint bar of light. I moved a little to find out where it was coming from, but moving made me feel worse than ever and I groaned. Then there was a shuffling noise.

"Feeling sick, ain't yer?" a voice said softly, just beside me.

"Mm," I muttered. "And my head – it aches . . ."

"It's that gas 'e give us," the voice said. It wasn't Nellie, I was sure of that. They gave you gas when you had a tooth out, but if I was at the dentist why was it so dark and cold? Something had gone dreadfully wrong, but I couldn't work out what it was.

"Where am I?" I asked. "And who are you?"

"I'm Dick," said the voice. I could dimly see a shape squatting beside me on the ground. "It'll go off after a bit – the sick feeling. Try sittin' up. That's wot I did."

"Have you had gas, too?" I asked, starting to heave myself up.

"Not 'alf . . . felt as sick as a dog when I come round. 'Ere, I thought you two would never wake up."

"Two?" I frowned. My head was still pounding, but I could see a bit better now. The figure beside me was wearing something white.

"Yer sister . . . look, don't you remember nothin'?"

"Flora," I muttered. Suddenly it all came back to me. "The hansom . . . we got into the hansom and then . . . where is she?"

"All right, all right. She's over there . . . she'll be round in a minute. 'E got me too," he went on, putting his hand on my arm. "With a pad of something from a bottle. I was just goin' under the archway – "

"The doves," I whispered. "Now I know who you are. You came and took the doves – "

"That's me," the boy nodded. I could see his head move now, and a glimmer of white teeth as he grinned. "I know who you are, too. I seen yer watching me. Yer was followin' me and all . . ."

"You knew," I muttered.

"'Course I did," he said in a matter of fact way. "Thought I'd lost yer by St Paul's, till yer bobbed up again in the shop." At that moment I heard Flora groan close beside me, and I scrambled over to her.

"Where am I?" she murmured. "I feel as if I'm going to be sick . . ."

"I did too," I said. "It'll stop soon."

"And my head hurts. William – what's that funny noise? And why am I lying on the floor?"

"Just try to sit up," I said, putting my arm round her. For a moment she hung on to me, peering into the creaking gloom, and then I felt her grip tighten on my arm.

"Who's that – over there? It's not him, is it?" I felt a shudder go through her.

"It's all right," I said quickly. "That's Dick . . . the boy we were following."

"He's here . . . ?" Flora whispered.

"I don't understand it myself yet," I frowned. "But that Chinese man caught him, too."

"We've been kidnapped, haven't we?" Flora whispered after a moment. She was still hanging on to me.

"It looks like it," I said. I shot a glance over my shoulder to where Dick was squatting on the ground, and he came over and knelt beside us. "This is Flora," I said.

"Pleased ter meet yer," he said, as though we were at a tea party. "I seen yer before, of course. Through the window."

"He knew we were following him all the time," I explained.

"You feeling better now?" Dick asked. Flora shook her head.

"I still feel sick. And I'm cold . . . I wish I was at home instead of here in this awful place." She started to shiver. "That Chinese man . . . he had something in a bottle. I couldn't breathe – "

"Gas, that's what that was," Dick said in a low voice. "'Ere, take this." He unwound the muffler from round his neck and passed it over to Flora. "We can jump up and down in a bit, get warmer that way." He looked over towards the bar of light. "I reckon this is the hold – where they've slung us."

"The hold," I muttered. "Of course . . . that's why we're rocking about. And that noise . . . we're on a ship – "

"You mean we're at sea?" Flora gasped. Dick shook his head.

"Moored up. Somewhere down Limehouse way, I shouldn't wonder."

"But what – " Flora began, and then stopped as we heard a clock beginning to strike somewhere in the distance.

"Six o'clock," Dick whispered, as the last chime faded away. "It'll be daylight soon, I reckon."

"You mean we've been here all night?" Flora said, leaning forward.

Dick nodded, and I saw that he was right. Already the early morning light had begun to find its way through chinks and crannies in the hold. I could make out the shape of a ladder now, leading up to the strip of light, and see that the lumpy outlines beside us were coils of rope. Dick's face was growing clearer too. I noticed that he wasn't wearing his cap, which made him look younger, although I guessed that he must be a year older than me. He was whistling softly under his breath.

"I suppose you tried the hatchway," I muttered.

"'Course I did, before you opened yer eyes," he replied cheerfully. "Locked in nice and tight we are." He leant forward, jerking his thumb towards the pile of bales that were just visible, lashed together along one side of the hold. "I tell yer one thing," he went on in a low voice. "That there cargo down there – I reckon Mr Rolandson wouldn't 'alf like ter know about that."

"Samuel," Flora breathed. "Then you do know him."

"'Course I know 'im," Dick nodded.

"Look," I cut in, "don't you think you'd better tell us everything you know. Now. Before that Chinese man comes down here. We've been trying to find Samuel ever since we got back on Sunday, and we still don't understand a thing that's going on."

"We thought at first that you'd stolen the doves," Flora said, looking at him.

"Stolen 'em!" Dick grinned. "Don't be daft. 'Course I 'adn't stolen 'em. It was your Guvnor as give me the job of fetching 'em, that's all."

"When?" I asked.

"Saturday it must 'ave been. Saturday morning." He stopped and looked at us both, sucking in his cheeks.

"Go on," I said.

"Silent," he whispered after a moment, scrambling closer to us. "Silent as the grave. That's wot 'e said. Your Guvnor. Made me swear it, too." He spat on his finger and drew it across his throat. "'Fetch and carry, but don't you breathe a word to a living soul, Dick my boy, else we'll all be done for.'"

I stared at him, imagining Samuel saying the words and putting his hand on Dick's shoulder as he spoke.

"It must be deadly serious," I muttered. "Worse than we guessed."

"'E's a bad un, all right," Dick nodded solemnly. "An out and out bad 'un."

"The Chinese man, you mean?" Flora said, with a shudder. But Dick shook his head.

"That one ain't nuffin," he said. "Just doin' wot 'e's told, see. It's the other one . . . the one wot your Guvnor's after. 'E's the one wot's 'ad us brought 'ere . . ." He stopped and shot a quick look towards the hatchway. But there was no sound.

"Look, you must tell us," I said, leaning forward. "I know you swore, but if Samuel was here he'd understand. We're all in it together now. He'd want you to tell us." Dick gazed at me for a moment and then looked at Flora. At last he nodded.

"Reckon you're right," he said.

"Well who is he?" I asked. "This man that Samuel is after . . ."

Dick looked towards the hatchway again and then moved closer to us.

"Nemo, that's wot they call 'im," he said in a low voice.

"Nemo," I muttered. The name meant nothing to me.

'"We've got ter catch 'im this time, or London won't be safe from – from 'is evil trade' . . . that's wot the Guvnor said." He paused, and a shadow seemed to pass over his face. After a moment he went on. "But 'e's a wily one, that Nemo. Slippery as an eel, I reckon. And it seems as though 'e's got wind of something. That's why 'e sent his stooge to fetch us."

"That's the same one who was watching our house," I muttered, beginning to understand.

"You seen 'im before then?" Dick asked.

"On Friday night," I nodded. "The night before we went away." Dick gave a low whistle.

"And on Saturday the Guvnor went away, too," he said. "That's 'ow 'e gave 'im the slip. But that Nemo won't stop at nothin' ter find out where 'e is."

"But I still don't understand," Flora cut in. "Where is Samuel?" But this time Dick shook his head.

"Best yer don't know that," he said quietly. "'Cos wot yer don't know yer can't tell." I frowned. "Stands to reason," he went on. "Nemo will be 'ere before long, and the first thing 'e's goin' ter try to find out is where the Guvnor is. It was you two 'e was after all along, not me at all. I think that 'e took me by mistake." Flora was staring at him and looking more baffled than ever.

"The old man in the bookshop wouldn't tell us where Samuel was either, although we were sure he knew," she said. "He just talked about crumpets all the time and then he locked us in, didn't he, William? If I hadn't found the trap door we'd still be . . ." She stopped. Dick was looking at her thoughtfully.

"Reckon you made a mistake there," he said slowly, and shook his head. "Yer'd 'ave been safer where you was." Flora put her hands up to her face. "I 'eard yer come into the shop," Dick went on. "We both did . . . Mr Partridge and me. And when 'e found out I'd seen yer the night before as well 'e was in a proper taking. 'Them poor young things, all alone in that 'ouse,' 'e said. 'Something must have gone wrong. We'd best get word to Mr Rolandson. You take them doves straight back to 'im Dick, and tell 'im ter get up 'ere directly. I'll keep them in the shop till 'e arrives.' "

"He sent you to fetch Samuel?" I said.

"Gave me money for a cab and all," Dick nodded. "Only I got nabbed, same as you. And 'ere I am."

"He was waiting for Samuel to arrive," I said, looking at Flora in dismay. "Don't you see? All the time we were there he was expecting Samuel to arrive at any moment . . . and then he locked us in because he knew we'd be safe in the shop while he went to find out what had happened."

"Samuel must have come to find us," Flora whispered after a moment. "And now he won't know where we are. Oh William, if only I hadn't found that trap door."

"We've done everything wrong," I groaned.

"Not yer fault," Dick said gruffly. "I'd 'ave done the same meself I shouldn't wonder." He gave a lopsided grin.

"I still don't understand about the doves," I muttered after a moment. Dick put his head on one side and looked at me.

"Aintcha guessed yet?" He said. There was quite a long silence. And then Flora gave a little gasp. I turned my head and looked at her.

"Messages," she whispered. "Samuel was using them to send messages. Wasn't he?" Dick nodded.

"And I'll tell yer something else . . ." He began.

But at that moment we heard above us the soft pad of footsteps coming along the deck towards the hatchway.

CHAPTER TEN

In which we dispatch a message and come face to face with Nemo . . .

Dick cocked his head to one side. The footsteps were coming closer.

"You'd best lie doggo and leave the talking to me," he muttered, scrambling away from us into the deeper shade on the far side of the hold. "Don't say nothin' . . ."

Then the strip of light above our heads widened, and the trap door was hauled open.

The early morning light flooded into the hold and for the first time I could see our prison clearly. Flora was huddled beside me, her face turned towards the open hatchway, and on the other side Dick squatted against one of the coils of rope that littered the floor. Beyond us, stretching away into the shadows, were linen covered bales stacked against each side of the boat.

For a moment the figure stood framed in the hatchway and we could hear him talking to someone on the deck in a rapid, chattering voice. The next instant he was coming swiftly down the steps towards us.

He lifted the lantern he was holding and surveyed us all in silence. We certainly looked a sorry sight, our faces pale and streaked with dirt and our clothes all crumpled and untidy, but his face was expressionless as he pattered silently over to one of the beams that ran overhead and hung the light on it. It was Dick who broke the silence.

"'Ow long you goin' ter keep me down 'ere?" he asked. "You got no right. I wanna go 'ome now . . . my muvver won't 'alf be worrying about me."

The Chinese man finished fixing the lantern and turned to look at Dick.

"No speak of mother," he said. "Now have tea to drink and eat bread. Master come later."

"Don't want no tea," Dick said defiantly. "I wanna go 'ome . . . I told yer . . . me muvver – "

"You speak of mother you get whipping," he said, suddenly drawing a bamboo cane from his belt and swishing it nastily in the air, so that Dick shrank back against the coil of rope. "Children must eat," he went on with an evil smile. "Master's orders." He looked at each of us in turn, making cuts in the air with his cane, until Flora gave a gasp and buried her face in the stuff of my jacket. I put my arm round her.

"All right, all right," Dick muttered. "No need ter get so uppity. I only asked . . ."

He took a step towards Dick, but at that moment his companion appeared down the hatchway carrying a tin tray with three mugs on it and some slices of bread and butter. He was younger than the one who had kidnapped us and his face was almost gentle, I thought, as his gaze flickered for a moment towards Flora and me. Then the first man said something that sounded like an order, and the next instant he had bolted up the steps again and vanished through the hatchway.

"Children not pleased with tea?" The other one leered, as none of us moved. His slant eyes didn't waver, but the cane cut through the air again.

"Yes," I muttered, eyeing it as it swished closer. "Thank you."

"Drink tea now, young sirs, Missy. Masters orders," he nodded, folding his arms.

I was afraid that he meant to stay and watch us, but as soon as I had nudged Flora and handed her one of the mugs he gave a satisfied nod, and tucking the cane back into his belt he padded over to the hatchway and disappeared up the steps. The hatch was slammed shut and we heard the quick thud of feet above our heads and the sound of voices fading away.

Dick was still crouched by the coil of rope.

"Are you all right?" I asked. He looked across at me and gave a quick grin.

"Not 'arf," he nodded. "Things is looking up, I'd say."

"Looking up?" Flora exclaimed. "After he nearly hit you with that stick of his . . . and now he's gone away and locked us up again. And the Master's coming. You heard what he said . . ." She broke off with a shiver.

"Real moanin' Minnie, aintcha?" Dick said, grinning at her cheerfully. "Look on the bright side. We've got tea and something to eat. And a light. Best of all, we've found out that Nemo ain't 'ere yet. That gives us time to think." He picked up one of the mugs and held it between his hands.

"Think about what?" Flora asked. "We can't possibly escape if that's what you mean – "

"I didn't say escape exactly, now did I?" Dick said. He took a gulp of tea and wiped the back of his hand across his mouth. "This ain't 'alf bad," he went on. "Go on, drink it . . . warm yer up."

"Well what did you mean then?" I asked after a moment. The tea was hot and sweet. I took another mouthful and began to feel better. "About not escaping exactly . . ." Dick didn't answer at once, but drained his mug and put it back on the tray. Then he glanced towards the hatchway and moved closer to us.

"There's something yer don't know yet," he said in a low voice. "Something I was goin' ter tell yer . . ."

"About the doves?" I said. Dick nodded. Then he picked up a

piece of bread and butter and carefully began tearing the crust off it while Flora and I watched him.

"Could be the ace card, yer might say," he said, glancing towards the hatchway again.

"Go on," Flora said breathlessly. Dick leant forward.

"Remember I told yer how that stooge got me just when I was on me way back to the Guvnor? Well I was taking the doves wiv me, wasn't I?" He put the bread and butter back on the tray and looked at us. For a moment there was silence.

"The doves," I murmured, hardly daring to believe my ears.

"'Ad 'em in a bit of silk net and wrapped in a cloth down me front," Dick nodded. "Like the Guvnor showed me. You'd 'ave thought they would 'ave found them, but the little blighters was still there when I come to meself again, and right as trivets."

"You mean they're here?" Flora gasped. "Here on the ship?"

"And not squashed nor nothing," Dick grinned. "You want ter see?" Without waiting for an answer he bounded over to the other side of the hold and came back carrying his cap.

Flora and I watched as he carefully unfolded the cloth that was arranged inside it, and there, nestled together under the silk net we could see the three doves. Of course they were used to being kept in the dark and in a small space like a pocket, because Samuel had trained them to work with him in his magic act, and that's the way he hides them. All the same, they'd been there a long time. I couldn't really believe that they were still alive and unhurt. But when I put my finger out to touch them I felt that they were warm and their hearts were beating as I gently ruffled their breast feathers.

It seemed like a miracle. By the light of the lantern I saw that Flora's eyes were shining, and Dick had a grin that stretched from ear to ear.

"Reckon they could find their way home?" He asked.

"They might . . ." I looked at Flora.

"If it's not too far," she nodded.

We were all thinking the same thing. If we could hit upon a way to release the doves we could let Samuel know where we were. And then there would be a chance, just a slim chance, that he'd be able to rescue us before Nemo arrived. For a moment I felt a surge of hope, until I saw the look on Flora's face.

"It's no good, William," she said, shaking her head. "Samuel's not at home. You know he isn't."

"I wouldn't be too sure of that," Dick said softly. We both looked at him. "Chances are 'e *did* go back 'ome last night, 'oping you was there . . ."

"Of course," I muttered. "As soon as he found we weren't in the shop that's the first place he would have looked." Dick nodded and sucked in his cheeks.

"And if this 'ere wherrie slipped in last night just before we was taken aboard 'e may not know it's docked. And 'e won't know that Nemo's on 'is way down 'ere neither . . . that's why we must try to get word to 'im." I frowned.

"How do you know this is a wherrie?" I said, after a moment. Dick didn't answer. "And earlier," I went on, "when we were talking, you said we were moored up at Limehouse. How did you know that?" By then Flora was looking at him curiously as well. But a stubborn expression had come over Dick's face and he shook his head.

"Waste of time this is," he said. "Talking . . . That Nemo could be here any time. So wot do you say, both of yer? Is it worth a try or not?"

"Of course it is," Flora said, shooting a quick glance towards the hatchway. I nodded.

"Anything's better than just waiting."

"We'll have to find something to write with," Flora said. "And paper."

"Thread and all," Dick nodded. "So as we can tie the messages to their legs . . . and we'll 'ave ter find a way to get them out."

"We'll think of something," Flora said, with sudden confidence. "But don't you think we ought to let them stretch their wings a bit now?" She touched the doves again with her finger. Dick shook his head.

"Best leave them where they are till we're ready," he said. "If they was to be found we ain't got no chance."

As he spoke he covered the doves over again and folded the cap round them so that they were invisible. Then he carried them back into the shadows on the other side of the hold.

It must have been half past six by then, and suddenly there seemed to be a great deal to do. But at least we had a plan, and that was better than sitting and waiting, wondering what would happen next.

Flora divided up the rest of the bread and butter between us, and as soon as I'd eaten my share I started to turn out my pockets, laying everything down on the tray so that the others could see. Nellie's always going on about the number of things I carry around with me, particularly my pen knife, which she seems to imagine will open up one day of its own accord and cut my leg in half. But as I keep telling her you never know when something will come in handy.

There was a conker on a string, and the change from the two sovereigns that Samuel had given me as well as Nellie's half crown; a half eaten humbug rolled up in a screw of paper, two marbles, my pen knife and the tram tickets from our ride the day before. If we separated the string into strands it would do to tie the messages to the doves' legs, but the paper around the humbug was too sticky to write on, and even though I dived into the deepest corners of my trouser pockets I still couldn't find a pencil.

"We could use the tram tickets," Flora said. "But that's not much use if we haven't got anything to write with. Are you sure,

William? About the pencil? You had one on the train. We were playing noughts and crosses . . ."

I rocked back on my heels, frowning and trying to remember. Nellie had gone to sleep in the corner, her bonnet sliding over one eye, and Flora had been cross because I'd won every time. It seemed twenty years ago instead of just two days.

"Your jacket!" She squealed suddenly, and so loudly that I leant across and clapped my hand over her mouth. We both looked up at the hatchway, but there was no sound from above and after a moment I let her go. She made a lunge at me, and I pushed her away and began searching feverishly through my jacket pockets.

It was still there, the little leather bound notebook that Samuel had given me last Christmas, with the pencil fitted into the spine so that it wouldn't get lost. I pulled it out triumphantly and laid it down on the tray.

"That's everything," Flora said excitedly. "Pencil, paper and string. Oh, the precious doves . . ."

"Only trouble is," Dick said, coming back from an exploration of the hold, "there ain't no way to get them out. No window nor nothing . . . except that hatchway." He squatted down beside us and began to whistle under his breath.

"There must be a way," Flora said firmly. Dick didn't answer.

I stared up at the hatchway and tried to think. The strip around it had been the only light we'd seen until the Chinese man brought the lantern, but I realised that it was no longer visible. I stood up and began taking off my jacket.

"What are you doing?" Flora asked.

"I've got an idea," I said, covering the lantern so that we were suddenly plunged back into darkness again.

All at once the bar of light around the hatchway was clear again, and brighter than before. It must be getting on for sunrise, I thought. I turned the other way and looked along the hold. Then I saw it. A tiny needle of light that pierced the gloom.

"Look!" I said excitedly. Dick stopped whistling.

"Blimey," he muttered. "'E's right."

"William's good at ideas," Flora said proudly.

Dick set off towards the light, feeling his way past the bales, while we waited. When he was close to it he gave a low call. I uncovered the lantern and Flora and I made our way towards him. I held the lantern up so that we could see.

There was a square opening, partly hidden by a coil of heavy rope and covered with some wire mesh. Dick had already clambered up on to the bales and was tugging the rope to one side, and as he moved it more light came in. I handed the lantern to Flora and climbed up beside him. Together we inspected the wire mesh. It was fixed to the frame with four catches, and after a great deal of wiggling we managed to push them back so that we could lift the mesh out. Then we took it in turns to peer up into the opening. We couldn't see any sky so I guessed that the shaft must have turned at an angle near the top, but the space was quite wide.

"What do you suppose it's for?" Flora whispered. By then she had put the lantern on the ground and was perched on the bales beside us.

"I think it's for air," I frowned, putting my hand into the space again. "There's quite a wind coming down it."

"Comes out on deck, if you ask me," Dick nodded. "But why don't the water come in?"

"I suppose there's a lid up there that they screw down when the weather's bad," I said.

"Could be wire at the top, too," Dick said, sucking in his cheeks.

Flora lay on her stomach and put her head into the shaft.

"Can you see anything?" I asked, when she'd been there for some time. She emerged again, looking rather tousled.

"No," she said in a low voice. "But I could hear things . . . voices, and a seagull. There was a horse going along, too."

"Then it must come out on deck," I said, looking at Dick. Flora nodded and put her finger to her lips.

"If we can hear them, they must be able to hear us," she whispered. We all looked towards the hatchway, but there was no sound of footsteps. "It sort of gets narrower half way up," Flora went on, leaning towards us. "But I think I could squeeze all of me in there, and maybe then I could see what happens at the top."

"Supposing you get stuck," I muttered. She shook her head.

"I won't. And if it's all right you could hand the doves to me one at a time and I could push them out."

"Well you're a plucky one and no mistake," Dick breathed, giving Flora an admiring look, so that she turned quite pink.

"Go on then," I whispered. "Only take care."

She began to wriggle into the shaft, and in a moment all we could see was her feet and the hem of her skirt. Dick and I waited, watching her boot heels rise, so we knew she was standing on tip toe. The seconds ticked by. I looked over my shoulder towards the hatchway again. If the Chinaman came down now, I thought, we'd be done for. After what seemed like a long time Flora's boot heels came down on to the top of the bales again and she wriggled out and dropped in an untidy heap beside us.

"It's all right," she said. "I can't exactly see out, but I put my arm up and felt, and there's an edge round the corner and then just nothingness." I looked at Dick.

"What do you think?" I whispered. He frowned and peered up into the shaft once more. Then he nodded.

"Sooner we can release them doves the better," he muttered.

The next thing was to write out the messages we were going to tie to the doves' legs.

It took some time to decide what we ought to say.

"We don't even know where we are," I frowned, looking across at Dick who was sitting on the steps leading up to the hatchway, keeping Cavie. "It's no use just putting 'On a wherrie on the Thames' . . ."

"There must be hundreds of them," Flora nodded. Dick sucked in his cheeks.

"If the Guvnor didn't see it come in he could search for a week and not find us," he muttered. For a minute or two we were stumped.

"You'd think the name would be written up somewhere," I muttered.

"I expect it is," Flora nodded. "But not down here, in the hold."

"There's something written 'ere," Dick said, pointing to the beam just above his head. "Come and 'ave a look."

I unhooked the lantern and went to see. It was a small metal plaque. On it was printed: SS Gloriana. Reg. Port of London.

"What a bit of luck," I grinned. "Why didn't you tell us at once?" Dick wiped his sleeve across his face and looked away.

"Couldn't quite make it out," he said.

"We ought to put our home address as well," I said, beginning to write. "In case the doves don't get back and someone finds them." I sucked my pencil again for inspiration, and went on. "Listen to this," I said, after a minute or two. "'To S. Rolandson, Esq. 25 Kennington Park Villas. From William, Flora and Dick. Prisoners on SS Gloriana. Please come . . .'" I looked up.

"Now put the time," Dick said, cocking his head to one side.

"Good idea," I nodded. "Six thirty a.m." Dick sucked in his cheeks and looked over towards the bales.

"Now put . . . 'cargo still aboard.'" I stared at him.

"What on earth for?" Flora asked. "It'll take ages to write all that out three times."

He came down the steps and squatted beside me, peering at the paper.

"Go on, write it," he said, ignoring Flora.

"But why?" I asked.

"'Cos it's important," he said in a low voice. "That's why. Look, yer don't know nothin' about Nemo and wot 'e does," he said with sudden passion. "But I do. And this is wot the Guvnor's after, wot's stacked up 'ere. If 'e's not told it's aboard Nemo will get clean away – " I wanted to ask what was in the bales, but Flora cut in.

"If it's going to help Samuel you'd better write it," she said. "And do hurry, William. That man could be back at any minute."

"All right," I nodded, seeing that she was right.

By the time I had written the three notes Flora had separated the strings into strands, and we were ready to tie them on to the doves' legs. Dick had kept the crusts from his bread to give them, but we couldn't decide whether we should feed them or not. If we gave them too much to eat they wouldn't want to fly; on the other hand they might be weak from lack of food. Birds have to eat very often to keep their strength up, so Samuel says, and they hadn't had a crumb of food since the day before. In the end we gave them a little of the bread out of the palms of our hands, just to keep them going.

Tying the notes to their legs was the most difficult part. I had folded them up very small, but it was a fiddly business. One of us had to hold the bird, while one twisted the paper round, and the third tied the message on with the string. It took a long time, but at last they were ready to fly. We made our way back down to the end of the hold and stood, looking at one another for a moment.

"You'll have to do it," I said to Flora. "You're the only one who can get up the shaft."

"We'll keep our fingers crossed for yer," Dick told her as she climbed up on to the bales. My dove was blinking a little, and turning its head from side to side. I gave it a quick kiss, for luck and then put it into Flora's hands. She disappeared into the shaft, and we heard her grunting. Then there was a sound of fluttering and scrabbling, and after that silence. I held my breath and looked at Dick.

"It works," Flora whispered, bobbing out of the shaft again. "It's flown . . . I could hear it go. Quick, give me the next one."

It seemed to take ages, and all the time I was afraid that the hatchway would be flung open and that we would be discovered.

Flora had just taken the last dove from Dick and wriggled up into the shaft again when we heard the sound of footsteps above us, and the thump of something being put down heavily on the deck. I started to tug at her boot heels to warn her. As I did so the faint beating of wings came wafting back down the shaft, and a second later Flora tumbled out on to the bales and landed at my feet.

"Someone's there," she whispered.

The footsteps passed overhead as we raced back to the other end of the hold. But the hatchway didn't open, and after a moment there was silence again.

"That was a close shave," Dick whispered. "Do you think they might 'ave seen?"

"I don't know," Flora breathed. "All that really matters is that the darlings have flown . . . all of them. It was wonderful! I felt like Noah in the Bible. He sent a dove, didn't he?"

We were quiet for a while, imagining the doves winging their way across the roofs of London towards Kennington. Then I grinned.

"You don't look much like Noah," I told Flora. "Your face is all covered with smuts. Here, take my handkerchief."

"Must I?" She screwed up her nose. "I hate all that spitting and rubbing."

"You don't want them to guess though, do you?" I said, pushing the handkerchief into her hand.

"Oh all right," she said, giving a quick dab here and there and then handing it back to me.

"We couldn't 'ave done it without yer," Dick said suddenly, leaning forward. "You wos the only one as could get into that tunnel. Catch me climbing up there . . . Not blooming well likely!"

"Oh I don't know," Flora said, wriggling a little. "You helped as well, you know. It was your idea in the first place. Wasn't it, William?"

"Yes, it was," I said thoughtfully. "As a matter of fact I don't know what we'd have done if you hadn't been here."

"It was lucky for us that you were," Flora nodded. We were both looking at Dick by then. He wiped his sleeve across his face and gave an embarrassed grin.

"Ger'off!" he muttered. Then a shadow seemed to pass across his face and his expression changed. "Come to that, it ain't over yet," he said in a low voice. "Not by a long chalk."

Suddenly the excitement of having dispatched the doves had gone, and the uncertainty of what was to come brought back the sinking feeling to the pit of my stomach.

"What is in those bales?" I asked, breaking the silence that had fallen amongst us. But Dick shook his head.

"I can't tell yer that," he said. "So don't ask me no more. I've told yer most everything else – "

"Except where Samuel was hiding," Flora cut in.

"And we've guessed that anyway," I muttered. "Or near enough. Samuel was somewhere down here, watching for the Gloriana to come in, wasn't he? And as soon as it did, then he was going to send one of the doves with a message . . . you were to collect the dove and take it to Mr Partridge." I paused, but Dick didn't answer me, just sat there twiddling with his cap.

"If we know that much, why can't you tell us what's in the bales," Flora asked, leaning forward.

"Because it's too dangerous," he said with sudden fierceness. "That's why."

"But *you* know," I said.

126

"It's different for me," Dick muttered. "You two didn't ought to be mixed up in this at all, and if you 'adn't come 'ome . . ." He broke off. "Why did yer come back anyway?"

"Because Nellie's sister was ill." Flora explained about Rose and the telegram and Dick listened, sucking in his cheeks. "But it all really began with Chang," she added at last. "And I still don't understand where he comes into all this – "

"Or Mr Partridge" I said. But Dick had turned away. The shadowed, haggard look had come back to his face and he was staring down the hold as though he could see something terrible in the darkness there.

"What is it?" I whispered, leaning towards him. I think I realised for the first time then how afraid he was. He spun round and grabbed my wrist.

"'E'll try to make yer tell," he said, his voice hoarse. "That's wot 'e'll do . . ."

"Nemo . . ." Flora breathed. Dick nodded.

"But yer mustn't say nothin' . . . no matter wot 'e does."

"It's all right," Flora said after a moment. "We won't. Truly we won't."

I swallowed. Suddenly it was as though he was amongst us already, making the darkness deeper. I wanted to say that perhaps the doves had reached home by then, and that maybe Samuel had found them and was on his way to rescue us. But the words didn't come.

Dick didn't say anything else. He went and sat on the coil of rope on the opposite side of the hold and tipped his cap over his eyes. After a while we heard him whistling softly under his breath.

Some time after that we began to hear noises. At first it was the tread of feet passing backwards and forwards above our heads. There was creaking, too, and between the creaks the clatter and crash of heavy objects being thrown down and trundled from one side of the deck to the other. There were voices as well, and all talking in Chinese.

Dick sat up and pushed back his cap.

"Something's goin' on," he muttered. "There must be a dozen of them up there."

"Samuel – " Flora began. Dick shook his head.

"That ain't the Guvnor. If you ask me . . ."

But he didn't get any further, because at that moment the voices above us were suddenly silenced, and we heard the tread of a heavier pair of feet coming towards the hatchway and a sudden, sharp command. The hatchway was flung open and brilliant sunlight flooded in on us, making us blink. Then the two Chinese men swarmed down the steps, and seizing us by our arms they pulled us to our feet and pushed us together until we were standing, facing towards the hatchway.

We saw him then, outlined at first against the sky; a tall, dark figure who blotted out the sun. For a moment there was silence. Then he leant forward to look at us and I heard myself give a gasp.

I had seen that face before. It was the face of the man in Samuel's photograph.

CHAPTER ELEVEN

In which we come ashore and Nemo
reveals his power . . .

Nemo came slowly down the steps into the hold and stopped in front of us.

I felt Flora slip her hand into mine, but I dared not look at her. Instead I stared down at the shiny black crocodile shoes and neat grey spats, and the line where his trousers ended, knowing that if I lifted my head my expression might give me away. One look had been enough, though, and I knew then, beyond any doubt, that it was the same man whose picture I had seen in Samuel's desk. He must have been Samuel's friend once, I thought, and now he was his enemy. It was very still in the hold now, and the thought circled round and round in my head. I could hear Flora breathing quickly beside me, and from a long way off, it seemed, the sound of voices chattering softly above our heads.

Then he spoke.

"You fool. You incompetent, bungling, half witted fool."

I thought he meant me, and I looked up in spite of myself. But his gaze went past me towards the two Chinese. The one who had kidnapped us in the hansom had Dick by the collar and was twisting his arm behind his back, but I saw his grip slacken and for a moment a look of fear shot across his face.

"Master . . ." He began.

"These were not my instructions," Nemo said, in the same quiet, icy voice. "I told you to find them and bring them to the house."

"Not my fault, Master," the man babbled, letting go of Dick and dropping suddenly to his knees. "This one . . ." All at once he was turning to look at the younger one who was holding Flora and me, and I saw him point a trembling finger in his direction. Nemo's lips curled back in contempt.

"Silence," he said. "Do you think you can deceive me? This is your doing. And you know the punishment for those who disobey my orders."

"Master . . . Master . . ." His voice had turned into a shriek, and his head was bowed to the floor.

Nemo looked down at him as though he was a black beetle that had run across his path. Then, turning towards the hatchway he barked out an order in Chinese, and the next moment two others appeared, and seizing the trembling man bundled him up the steps.

The blood surged in my ears and I felt Flora grip my hand more tightly as his screams echoed back down the hold. For an instant I turned and looked over my shoulder at the young Chinese man who still held us; his face was blank, without expression, but his gaze rested on Nemo, and I thought that I saw a flicker of something like hatred in his slanting eyes.

Then, for the first time, Nemo turned his attention to us. He was a tall man, taller than Samuel, and as he looked down at us from what seemed a great height, I noticed that his eyes were sunk deep in his skull, neither blue nor brown, but a strange, glittering grey.

"You are coming with me," he said. "But not just yet. At present there is work to be done." He paused. "I have no alternative but to tie you all up."

"Look, Mister," Dick cut in, taking a step forward. "Can't yer let me go. I don't know nothin' about none of this and I want ter go back to me muvver . . . I done nothin' wrong. Honest I 'aven't . . ."

"Stay where you are," Nemo said, "and hold your tongue." His voice was quiet, but Dick didn't move again. "You are English children," he went on after a moment, and his glittering gaze rested on each of us in turn. "You do not snivel like these Chinese scum. Theirs was once the greatest civilization on earth, but they threw it all away, and look at them now ... whining and whimpering like dogs." He shot a contemptuous glance towards the young Chinese man who still held Flora and me. When he spoke again his voice had become very gentle. "None of you will be hurt if you do as you are told. Do you understand me? You are too valuable for that. You have things to tell me, all of you. Things that I want to know. Only if you call out, or try to escape will you be punished." He paused for a moment, and then nodded to the young Chinese. "Tie them up," he said. "And put them over there, out of the way."

It had been very quiet in the hold while Nemo spoke. Now I glanced at Flora and saw the look of hopelessness on her face. I suppose all three of us knew then that our plan had failed, and that our only chance of escape had gone. It was an hour since we had pushed the doves out of the shaft, but even if Samuel had found them the very minute they arrived home, I didn't see how he could possibly get to the wherrie before Nemo took us away. And once we had left the riverside he would never be able to find us.

As soon as the young man had bundled us into the corner beside the steps leading up to the hatchway and had started to bind our wrists and ankles together with rope, Nemo turned away and began issuing orders through the hatchway. Dick submitted silently to having the rope bound round him, although he managed to wink at us once behind the man's back. But when it came to Flora's turn I saw her open her mouth to protest, and I had to nudge her quickly to tell her to keep quiet.

"It's no use," I whispered. "You'll only get hurt."

131

Out of the corner of my eye I saw Dick nod in agreement, and after that Flora stayed quiet. I was glad that it wasn't the other one tying us up, although thinking about what might have happened to him made me feel sick. But the young one was almost gentle and when he'd finished with the knots I found that there was plenty of room to wiggle my wrists inside the rope. So much room that I frowned and shot a quick glance at the others. At that moment Nemo came back down the steps and leant over the rail towards us.

"Turn them round to face the wall," he said.

"Yes, Master," the young man said.

We were sitting on the floor by then and unable to move, and my last glimpse of the hatchway was of something that looked like a huge stage property basket handed down the steps. Then the young man swivelled me round. As he bent down his head was close to ours.

"No speaky . . . no try to escape now," I heard him murmur very softly. "Maybe later, from house."

Just for a moment I wasn't sure that I'd really heard the words, but one glance at Flora showed me that I was right, and my heart leapt. The next instant Nemo's voice rang out again behind us.

"And tie something round their mouths. I don't want them talking to one another."

What happened next was something like a bad dream that won't end, as we sat in a row facing the wall, bound and gagged and unable to move much or speak, and not knowing where Nemo would take us or what was going to happen to us when we got there. Behind us we could hear the creak of baskets being handed down from the hatchway and the tread of feet on the boards of the deck. There seemed to be a great many people in the hold by then, chattering to one another as they worked at unloading the cargo and from time to time Nemo's voice rose clear above the rest as he gave out orders. I sensed that he was in a hurry to get the work finished. The words of the young Chinese man kept circling round in my head as I tried to work out whether he really meant to help us, or whether it was just a trick.

Little by little I managed to edge closer to Flora until our shoulders were touching. Out of the corner of my eye I could just see a patch of Dick's white apron, and after a while I heard him beginning to hum softly through the gag, so softly that Nemo couldn't hear. But I knew then that in spite of everything he was telling us not to give up hope, because Samuel might, he just might arrive in time.

It was soon after that, I suppose, that I first noticed the bale to the left of where I was sitting. Someone had put the lantern down beside it, just a few inches away from me, and I realised that it had split open so that I could see what was inside. I stared at it intently. Dick had said that the cargo was dangerous, but all I could see was white powder which trickled slowly out from the gash in the bale and made a little heap beside the lantern. It certainly wasn't gunpowder, I decided, because gunpowder was grey. But it had a strange smell, and staring at it was beginning to make me feel sleepy.

Somewhere inside my head a voice was trying to tell me about the white powder and why it was so dangerous, but just as I thought I had the answer the voice kept floating away. I tried to think about Samuel instead. The thoughts went slowly round inside my mind and my eyes were so heavy that I could barely keep them open. Samuel had found the doves, I thought. He was unwrapping the note and reading it . . . running back into the house and up the stairs . . . out through the front door, and hailing a cab. My legs were heavy too . . . and that was strange, because my head was light now . . . as light as a balloon. Then the cab was rattling by, quite close, creaking and bumping. The driver gave a tug on his reins.

"Lift you in, young sir," he said.

"That one should sleep until we get there," Samuel said.

So it was me in the cab, I thought. The smallest cab I'd ever travelled in and all made of wicker work. Flora was beside me, but it was dark now and I couldn't see her. Besides, my eyes were closing as we bumped over the cobblestones. But I could hear Dick whistling again. Dick . . . I smiled to myself. 'Half a pound of tuppenny rice, half a pound of treacle . . ."

Then there was a voice.

"Wake up, William . . . Oh do, please, please wake up."

Through the mist of sleep I could hear the urgency in her voice and with an effort I opened my eyes. At first I saw only the wicker sides of the basket. Afterwards Flora's face was there, bending over me. She was very white and her eyes were wide with fear. There were other faces as well, Chinese faces, and as I sat up I thought at first that I must be still asleep and dreaming.

It was like a dream as I saw in an instant the cobbled courtyard, surrounded by low, brick buildings, and the spiked iron gate that shut out the world beyond. Steam and noise came from the buildings; the clatter of machinery and the sound of voices, and wherever I looked I saw Chinese people, some young and some old, in blue cotton trousers and soft black shoes, hurrying about with their pigtails flying as they went in and out of the buildings and up and down the iron stairways. We might have been in Shanghai or Pekin.

"Thank goodness you're awake," Flora breathed.

Before she could say anything else I was being half lifted, half dragged from the basket and my gag was being taken off. My legs felt wobbly, like cotton wool and my head was still muzzy with sleep, but after a moment I felt myself revive as great gusts of fresh air blew about my face. Above me I could hear the sound of flapping, like sails in the wind, and looking up I saw that lines and lines of washing were strung across the courtyard.

"It's a laundry," I muttered. Suddenly I was fully awake, and all that had happened came flooding back into my mind. "A Chinese laundry."

I looked round for Nemo, but there was no sign of him. And no way of escape from the courtyard; the Chinese must know that, too, because they were untying the ropes from around our wrists and ankles. I looked round for the young one, but his face wasn't amongst the ones who were untying us. Our plan has failed, I thought. Samuel hadn't come in time and now he would never find us.

"Where are we," I muttered, sidling up to Dick as soon as they had finished untying me and had turned to Flora.

"Limehouse," he mouthed back. "Remember, don't let on when we see Nemo . . . don't say nothin'."

"It doesn't matter now, does it?" I said emptily. "I know what was in those bales . . . and it's too late." But Dick grabbed my arm and held it ferociously.

"Don't yer give up now," he muttered. "Neither of yer . . ." His face was set in an obstinate line.

I turned my head away from him and stared up at the sky, taking great gulps of the fresh, cold air. Now that I was completely awake again my mind was racing and I was beginning to understand things more clearly. I understood about the white powder in the bales, and what it was that had sent me to sleep down there in the hold. I was beginning to understand what gave Dick the haunted look that came over his face from time to time, and I knew why Samuel had tried so hard to stop Nemo before the cargo could be unloaded. I thought I understood, too, where Chang fitted in and why he and Samuel had talked so late into the night.

And the worst of it was that now it was too late to do anything. We were Nemo's prisoners, and as they hurried us towards the gate on the far side of the courtyard I was more than ever afraid of the terrible danger that faced us all.

The gate was opened and we found ourselves looking into an

old, lined face the colour of a singed paper. I could see at once that he was different from the others. He wore a robe of figured silk, like Chang's, and he had a long, wispy beard that was greyish white. He bowed.

"Master waits," he said. "Children follow me."

Then we were in an alleyway. Ahead of us was another high gate, with spikes on top of it, and to our left the wall of a house. He led us through a side door, and then shut and locked it behind us.

A flight of stairs led up to the first floor, but before we reached them he turned instead into a small, bare room with a stone flagged floor and bars on the window. There was a table in the middle of the room, and on it was a bowl of water with a cake of soap and a towel.

"Children wash now, then eat soup. After that see Master," he said, in his cracked, sing song voice. He signalled towards the bowl of water, and then rang the bell beside the door twice. After a moment we heard footsteps and an old woman shuffled in, carrying a tray with a black iron saucepan on it and some bowls.

Washing has never been something I've cared for very much, but for once I was pleased to put my hands into the warm water, and when I'd splashed some of it on to my face and soaped the grime from my hands I felt better. The smell that was coming from the saucepan made me realise how hungry I was, and when the old woman had ladled the soup into the bowls I picked mine up at once, even though there was no spoon, and began to taste it. Flora looked at me in horror and wrinkled her nose.

"Chinese soup – very good," the old man said, and then, as though divining what was in her mind, he drank some himself from the ladle. "Not poisoned," he told her.

"But there's no spoon," she said.

"In China drink soup, not eat it," he replied, and then gave a little clap with his hands. "Chop chop. Master waits."

"May as well do as he says," I muttered to Flora. "It tastes all right."

As I drank the soup I was telling myself that Nemo couldn't make me say anything that I didn't want to, but the sinking feeling had come back into the pit of my stomach all the same as we followed the robed figure out of the room and towards the stairs. There had been no chance for us to talk to one another, and now we were being taken to Nemo.

"Remember, don't say nothin'," Dick managed to whisper to us as we reached the foot of the stairs. "And don't give up hope."

But there was no hope, I thought. Samuel would never find us here.

The old man pushed open the heavy, padded door at the top of the stairs and we found ourselves in a different world. The air hung heavy, with a smell that I recognised and which made me feel sick. It seemed to cling to me as I moved, and it was dark, so dark that all the curtains and shutters in the house must have been closed to keep the daylight out. Before the padded doorway swung shut behind us I could make out a hallway, with several doors opening off it, and in the heavy, brooding stillness there were soft footfalls, and someone coughed. Once a laugh rang out, making Flora jump beside me and grab my arm. The laugh was as eerie and unreal as the place we were in.

As we reached the next flight of stairs Flora stumbled and tripped on the bottom step.

"The front door," she whispered, as I helped her up. I shot a quick look over my shoulder. I could make out the outline of the doorway. Beyond it, in the street, a dog was barking. Then the old man was beside us.

"No escape from Master," the sing song voice murmured. A tall figure had lurched out of one of the open doorways and was standing, leaning against the wall, looking at us.

"Hello, young things," he said, in a jolly voice, and waved his top hat. "What are you doing here? Not the place for you," he added, suddenly becoming mournful and shaking his head. "Not the place at all . . ." Someone appeared beside him and he was taken back into the room again.

"Master waits," the old man murmured.

Nemo threw back his head and looked at us as we came into the room. The table he was sitting at was spread with a white cloth and there was a decanter of wine and a dish of walnuts in front of him. Behind his chair, at a respectful distance, stood the young Chinese man.

"Welcome to my house," Nemo said. "I have been expecting you since last night. Now that you are here I trust that you have been well looked after." He smiled, and his glittering gaze rested for a moment on each of us in turn. Then he snapped his fingers. "Very well, Lee Sun. You can go. You, too," he said, half turning in his chair. "Wait outside."

The young one bowed, and for a fraction of a second as he raised his head and looked towards us I saw a change in the blank expression of his face. It was the hint of a smile, no more. But it was enough, and without looking at the others I stared quickly down at the carpet in case I should betray the sudden flicker of hope that I felt. I heard the door open and close again, and then we were alone with Nemo.

"You are cleaner, certainly," he said after a moment. "And it was I who ordered the soup. So, you see, there is no need for any of you to be afraid."

I shot a swift, sidelong glance at the others. Dick had taken his cap off and was staring down at it, and Flora, who was standing next to me, was gazing over towards the window where the sun filtered through the closely drawn lace blinds. None of us spoke. Nemo gave a slight smile, and his fingers closed round the nut crackers. I hadn't noticed his hands until now, but I remember thinking that they looked very white, almost as white as the table cloth, and his fingers as they moved delicately amongst the walnuts, were long and curved, like the talons of a bird.

"I promised you that not a hair of your head should be harmed, and I have kept my word," he went on. "You are here, you see, safe and sound. You have clean hands and faces and your stomachs are full of the most excellent Chinese soup. So now you will do something for me in return. A small thing . . . a trifle. All you have to do is to answer my questions. You, young lady, what is your name?"

Flora edged closer to me and stared back at him without a word, tilting her chin. After a moment Nemo smiled again and transferred his gaze to me.

"You, then. You shall tell me what you are called, since your sister appears to have lost her tongue. She is your sister, I presume?"

It was hard to meet his glittering eye. I frowned and looked quickly down at the carpet. He gave a light sigh, and when I looked up again I saw that he was watching Dick, who stared up at the ceiling, his face quite blank.

"A silent pact," Nemo said gently. "I see. How foolish. And how ungrateful. But it will be no use, as you will discover. In truth, dear children," he went on in a soft voice that sent a shiver down my spine, "your silence tells me a great deal. More, perhaps, than I could have found out in half an hour of questions. It tells me that you have something you wish to hide."

The room had become very still, with a silence that stretched out and out, through the door and down the stairs, unbroken by footsteps or the sound of voices. We were in a cave of quietness. Then there came a sudden crack, so loud that I felt Flora jump beside me and saw her clap her hand over her mouth. On the table cloth the walnut shell lay shattered in pieces in front of Nemo.

"You see how easily it is done," he said. "A simple matter of knowing where to apply the pressure. And Hey Presto! All is revealed." He seemed almost to be talking to himself, and without looking up at us again he began to separate the pieces of shell from the kernel of the nut with his long, talon like fingers.

He was Samuel's enemy, I thought, watching his hands sweep the fragments of shell to one side. Soon he would start asking us questions. But still Nemo didn't speak. He poured himself some more wine and sipped it slowly, turning round and looking at the sunlight that filtered through the blinds. Sip after sip. The silence inched on and on and still he didn't look at us. Suddenly I couldn't bear it any longer. I wanted to shout and scream and beat the table in front of me. I wanted to hurl the walnuts through the window. I wanted most of all to tell him that I hated him. Anything would be better than this endless waiting. One of us would have to break the silence. One of us must . . . it couldn't go on like this. Dick wouldn't speak, I knew that. And Flora was too afraid.

Then it would have to be me. I would be the one to speak . . .

As though he had read my thoughts Nemo looked up and smiled at me, dusting the last of the walnut shell from his fingers with his napkin.

"And now," he said gently, "you will tell me your name."

"William," I answered readily, my voice sounding strange in my own ears. "My name is William."

"Good," he nodded. "Well, William Rolandson, so you have been the first to see reason and break that foolish pact. You shall be the spokesman for the others, and we will get on together quite comfortably, you and I. What is your sister's name?"

"Flora," I said.

"And the boy with the white apron who smells of fish?"

"That's Dick," I said. "He's an oyster seller." Nemo nodded in a most understanding way. His glittering gaze didn't waver now, but seemed to draw me closer to him. I no longer felt angry or afraid, and his voice had grown kind. It made me feel safe and warm inside, so that I wanted him to go on talking.

"My servants call me the Master," he smiled, speaking just to me so that everything else was blotted out. "But when I lived in England I had another name, many years ago. They called me Nemo then." I nodded. "You have heard that name, I see." He paused for a moment, and then sighed. "How strange that you should know my name. You see, it is almost twenty years since I was last in London. And now I can only stay for a short while, just long enough to finish what I came here to do. Then I shall be gone again, across the seven seas, back to the land where the sun rises beyond the white mountains. Nothing must delay my journey," he went on, leaning forward a little. "There must be no knot in the skein. My plan, you see, has been perfected over many years, William. Ah, England, land of my birth . . ." He smiled, and I smiled back at him. "When I was a young man, here in England, I was not known as the Master. Tell me, William, have you not heard your father speak of someone by the name of Nemo?"

"My father?" I frowned.

"Yes, we were friends then, Samuel Rolandson and I, when we served together as fellow officers. But we parted, he to go his way and I to go mine, and I haven't seen him since. Where is he now?"

"But Samuel isn't my father," I said. The words came without my having to think of them, as though it was some part of myself that spoke, the ordinary, everyday me who was used to explaining about Samuel being our Guardian. I had said nothing wrong, but all at once the glittering gaze seemed to flash fire.

"Not your father?"

"No," I said. "No . . ."

"You are deceiving me," Nemo said, his voice full of anger and reproach. "Come now, William. Tell me the truth. Samuel Rolandson is your father, and I want to know where he is."

"No," I cried, wishing that he would understand and not be angry with me any longer. "No, he's my Guardian, not my father.

Samuel adopted me when I was a baby – " I stopped. There was silence for a moment and then I saw him smile again.

"Your Guardian," he said softly. "I see. What a very truthful person you are, William. You didn't wish to deceive me in the smallest detail. I understand that now, and I believe that I can place perfect trust in you." He paused. "We are friends, aren't we? You and I?"

"Oh yes," I said.

"Then you will tell me the truth. You see, Samuel and I quarrelled many years ago, and now that I am in England I would dearly like to see him, to heal the rift between us and make amends, if I can. Do you understand?" I nodded. "By tomorrow evening I shall be gone again, never to return. How sad, how unbearably sad not to see him just once more. That is why I have been looking for him. But Samuel has vanished."

"I know," I said.

"My servants tell me that he left his house and they can find no trace of him. But you can help me, can't you? You know where he is." I frowned and shook my head. "You must know . . ."

"But we don't," I said. "We've been looking for him, too."

"I see," Nemo said slowly. "So that is why you went to Paternoster Court? You expected to find him there?" The glittering eyes seemed to probe and burrow into my mind. For a moment I wanted to resist, but that seemed stupid. Why not tell him everything. After all, he had said that we were friends. And he was the Master. "Yes, yes," he went on, as though he were answering my thoughts. "You may tell me all that you know. Look at me, don't try to turn your eyes away from mine. You went to the bookshop . . ."

Someone was shouting.

"Stop it! Stop it, I tell you. Leave him alone. William, you mustn't answer. It's lies . . . lies . . ." I frowned at the interruption.

"Go on," Nemo said, nodding at me. "You want to tell me, don't you?"

"Yes," I said. "Yes, I do – "

And then, from a long way off it seemed, I heard the thud of feet outside the door. The glittering gaze wavered and shifted. He was looking away from me, across the room, and in an instant I saw his face smoulder into sudden rage, and knew him again for what he truly was.

Then I was aware of Flora, staring at me as though I was a stranger to her, and of Dick, twisting his cap round in his hands. My teeth were chattering and a terrible, icy coldness had taken hold of me.

There was a knock at the door, and Nemo pushed back his chair.

CHAPTER TWELVE

In which the Bookseller returns, and Nemo makes a hurried exit . . .

It took him no more than a moment to open the drawer of the desk behind him and take out the revolver.

"Stay exactly where you are, all of you," he said in a low voice. "And keep quiet, or it will be the worse for you."

He crossed the room and stood with his back to the door, facing us, with the revolver cradled on his forearm.

"Well?" he asked through the door. "What is it, Lee Sun?"

From the other side we heard the sing song voice beginning to explain, and Nemo listened, his glittering gaze never wavering from us and the revolver held steady. After a moment or two he smiled, and then replied briefly in Chinese.

"A happy interruption after all," he said, his hand moving to the door knob. "Now I wonder, shall I allow you to meet my visitor? It would certainly be interesting . . ."

He broke off, and his glittering stare rested on me, as though he wanted to draw me back to him. But it was too late. I had so nearly given everything away, and now I hated him for what he had done to me. With an effort I turned my eyes away and stared instead at his hand which was curled round the gun like the talons of a great bird of prey. "I must never look at him again," I thought. "Never, never . . ."

"On second thoughts," I heard him say, "it will be better if you are all out of sight. You will have to wait in the next room until we can resume our interesting conversation. Lee Sun will wait with you, to make sure that you behave in a proper way."

As he spoke he opened the door and Lee Sun came into the room. Behind him we could hear footsteps coming up the stairs, and a voice speaking in English.

I lifted my head and looked at Flora and Dick, and a wave of relief swept through me. I knew whose voice it was, and I wanted to call out. But Lee Sun had taken the revolver and was waving to us to go towards the half open door which led into the next room.

"I promise not to keep you too long," Nemo smiled. "In the meantime not one word from any of you, or Lee Sun may have to use that thing."

For an instant as we went towards the door it came into my mind that I should double back, give just one yell. Then I felt Dick nudge against me and saw him shake his head. Anyway, Lee Sun was right behind us, and it wouldn't have been any use.

He had come to find us, I thought, sitting down on the chaise longue beside Flora and Dick in the shadowy room. Samuel had found our message after all and had somehow discovered where we were. Why else should the bookseller have come? And we were close to him, so close that we could hear his voice quite clearly through the door. But he didn't know we were there, and we had no way of telling him. Lee Sun was standing in front of us and the revolver was pointed in our direction. If only it had been the other one, I thought. The young one – then we might have had a chance. But he seemed to have disappeared.

"You bring good news, I hope," Nemo was saying. "Come in and sit down."

"Yes, thank you. No . . . I'll keep my gloves and muffler, if you don't mind. Cold weather indeed, a very sharp wind this morning. It quite makes one think of warm fires and crumpets, don't you agree? However, to business. I came immediately . . ."

"You have it?" Nemo asked, his voice suddenly sharp with greed.

"Not exactly. My dear Sir you must not be impatient. The matter is most delicate, as I have told you. There is someone else who wishes to purchase the – er – the volume . . ."

"I am aware of that. And you are aware that I am prepared to pay a high price for it. And to you for your services."

"Indeed, most generous. Well, I am happy to tell you that my client has agreed to sell to you."

"Excellent," Nemo replied. "You bring me good news, my friend."

"There is just one thing . . ."

"Well?"

"I understand that in view of the special circumstances surrounding this sale, my client wishes the exchange to take place at a particular place and at a particular time. He has asked me to give you this letter." There was silence for a moment, and then a ripping sound as Nemo slit open the envelope.

At first I had stared past Lee Sun towards the door, certain that all this was part of a plan Samuel had to rescue us, and that at any moment we would discover what it was. But now the conversation had taken a turn I didn't understand. Why, I wondered in bewilderment, were the bookseller and Nemo on such friendly terms? And what could be so important about the book they were discussing. After a moment we heard Nemo's voice again.

"Do you know what is in this letter? Is it some kind of trickery?"

"Trickery? In such a very public place. My dear sir, I hardly think that is likely. Indeed, it was to protect you both that the arrangements were made . . . to avoid any chance of trickery, you might say." He paused and cleared his throat. "My instructions are to find out whether you agree. If you do, then the sale can go ahead. And if not . . . forgive me, but I believe I am right in saying that this volume is unique. A unique collection of personal memoirs, and of extraordinary interest to you."

"You know quite well that is the case," Nemo replied, his voice suddenly harsh. "I have come half way across the world to obtain the book and I mean to have it before I leave England tomorrow night."

"In that case I can only advise you to accept the terms. Otherwise, I am afraid there are others – "

"One other, to be precise," Nemo cut in. "Fortunately one of them is dead ... of cholera, I was told. The other one would dearly love to get his hands on that volume, and to see me in hell at the same time."

There was silence for a moment. Then there came a rustle.

"Were you aware that two children visited my shop yesterday afternoon?"

In the pause that followed, the revolver in Lee Sun's hand seemed to waver before my eyes.

"I see that we understand one another," Nemo said, in slow, icy tones. "And since that is the case I may as well tell you that Samuel Rolandson will not dare to lay a finger on me now. I have made quite certain of that. Those children are to be kept out of harm's way until I leave England."

"A very wise precaution," the bookseller said. "It would be a pity if anything were to go wrong at this stage. And now, if you will excuse me, I have left a cab waiting outside. It has been a pleasure to do business with you, Sir. I trust that we shall meet again. And I will tell my client that you agree to his terms."

"Tell him I will not fail to be there," Nemo said. There were footsteps moving towards the door, and a click as it opened.

I felt sick. Sick with a hope that had twisted up inside me and turned into despair. Samuel had been betrayed by the bookseller who was supposed to be his friend. I didn't understand about the book, only that it was important, and now Nemo would escape from England taking it with him. And what would become of us?

Flora's head drooped on to my shoulder. I looked hopelessly towards Dick, but he didn't turn his head. He was slumped against the arm of the chaise longue, drumming his fingers against his knees and staring at the ground. Out of nowhere the thought came to me that he was no longer holding his cap. Then the door swung open.

"Very well, Lee Sun, you may bring them out now."

He took the revolver from him and put it back on top of the desk, saying something in Chinese as he did so. Lee Sun nodded and slipped out of the room, closing the door silently behind him.

"We shan't be disturbed again," Nemo said, sitting down at the table and pouring himself another glass of wine. "Come over here and stand in front of me. Dear me, how exceedingly glum you all look."

His glittering gaze rested on each of us in turn, and he smiled unpleasantly. I stared down at the table to where the letter lay, half tucked under the dish of walnuts. I could see the dark, sloping writing on the envelope and something blue sticking out of one corner.

"And just when all my plans are about to reach a glorious conclusion," he went on. "What a pity that you can't share my pleasure. You, young lady, you look as though you are about to burst into tears."

"I am not," Flora said defiantly, tilting her chin in the air. "But if I was it wouldn't be any wonder. You think you can do just what you want to us, don't you? Because we're your prisoners in this awful house . . . threatening us with a gun and frightening William almost to death – "

"Flora," I said, putting my hand on her arm, as I saw his eyes flash dangerously.

"Well he did," she said, shaking me off. "It was horrible. You went as white as chalk and you couldn't even hear me when I

148

shouted at you. And all because you want us to tell you where Samuel is," she went on, her voice rising as she looked at Nemo. "Why don't you believe us? We've been looking for him for two whole days and we still haven't found him . . . and it doesn't matter how long you keep us here we still can't tell you."

Nemo sat very still, his long white fingers locked together tightly in front of him. Only his eyes moved.

"That was your second outburst," he said in icy tones. "I shall have to find a way to curb your spirit. Tell me, did Samuel adopt you, too? Foolish, sentimental old woman that he is . . ."

"Samuel is the best and dearest person in the world," Flora cried in a choking voice. "And if you say anything else about him, I'll – "

"Look, Mister," Dick cut in quickly, taking a step forward. "Wot about me? I don't know nothin' about none of this. You 'eard wot the old geyser said. Two kids went into the shop . . .'e didn't say nothin' about me. I was just goin' back 'ome after leavin' me barrow in the courtyard, like I always do, and this fellow nabs me. Why don't yer let me go and 'ave done with it?"

"What? Let you go so that you can run straight to the nearest policeman and tell him that I am holding these two as my hostages? That would be very unwise of me."

"Well wot are you goin' ter do wiv us then?" Dick asked. "You can't keep us 'ere for ever." Nemo's lips curled back in a contemptuous sneer and his gaze swept over us again.

"We shall see about that," he said. "To tell you the truth I no longer care where Samuel Rolandson is. He will not find me here, and nor will he find you. By tomorrow night I shall have what I came to England for and be gone. But you . . . yes, all of you . . ." He paused, fingering the stem of his wine glass. "You know too much," he went on very quietly. "For instance, you know what kind of house you are in. You have smelt it, haven't you? And seen people acting strangely as you came up the stairs . . . Ah yes!" His eyes were on Dick and he nodded. "Yes, I see that you, for one, know very well what happens in this house."

"Well, and wot if I do?" Dick muttered, and looking at him I saw once again the haunted expression that had been in his eyes before.

"Just so," Nemo murmured. "And you can guess what cargo was unloaded from the Gloriana. Why don't you tell them, Dick?"

"He doesn't need to tell us," I cut in. "We all know now. It's opium, and you've smuggled it into England."

Dick shot me a quick look, and I saw Flora's eyes widen.

"That's what made you go to sleep in the hold," she whispered.

"Opium," Nemo nodded."You are quite right, William. It is made from poppies. White, waving, majestic poppies. In China, where the poppies grow they call it the happy flower and small wonder. Opium sends you to sleep and gives you the most beautiful dreams imaginable."

Flora shuddered, and I saw Nemo give an evil smile.

"Just so," he murmured. "A little more opium and all you will want to do is sleep and dream, dream and sleep. That is why those who have tried it can never bear to be without the pleasure which it brings. They crave it more than anything else in life. More than family or friends ... more even than food." He smiled. "The Chinese have destroyed themselves through opium. Now they are too weak and foolish to realise that only those who grow and sell it can profit by it."

Dick had begun to shake. I saw him steady himself against the table, but Nemo didn't seem to notice, and his voice went on.

"In England, where opium smoking is against the law, those who have acquired the habit must take their pleasures in secret, hounded always by the law of the land. And still they cannot do without it." He smiled again. "Oh yes, the precious poppy has made me rich. So you see now why the cargo of the Gloriana is so valuable and why I cannot possibly let you go. You would tell

Samuel, and he would go to the police. You have become a danger to me, and to everyone in this house."

He pushed his wine glass away from him and stood up.

"There will be no escape, I promise you," he went on, his voice quiet and cold, so that I felt a shiver run down my spine. "I have decided already what I shall do with you. Would you like to know?"

None of us answered him, but after a moment his voice went on.

"I will tell you just the same. You, Dick, will go and work in the laundry next door. It will make a pleasant change from selling oysters, and the obscurity of the place will mean that you will never be discovered, particularly with so many to guard you night and day. For you, young lady," he continued, turning to Flora, "I have planned a new life, too. You are to become the kitchen maid here in this house. Lee Sun will see to it that you work hard from dawn till dusk, sweeping and scrubbing and preparing the vegetables. Time will pass, and after a while you will grow used to the life, I daresay. You will forget all about Samuel. And you will learn not to shout, but to respect your elders; to be seen but not heard."

I had no idea how long we had been standing there listening to his voice, because time had ceased to have any meaning. But looking up at him now I knew in a flash that he was quite mad. He was sneering contemptuously down at Flora, but the look on his face was one that I hadn't seen before and it was as though he had turned to ice.

"Lee Sun!" he called, and the door opened at once. "Take them away."

Then Flora started to scream, and Lee Sun had taken her by the arm and was dragging her towards the door.

"William, William, help me!" she cried. I started to go to her, but Nemo's arm shot out across the table and held me fast. I saw Lee Sun put his hand over her mouth and twist one of her arms behind her back so that she was pinned against him.

"Let me go!" I shouted at Nemo, as his grip tightened on me.

"Stand still and be quiet," he said. "I have plans for you, too."

Another man had come through the door, but it wasn't the young one.

"Don't give up 'ope," Dick cried. "Don't never – "

The words were stopped by the hand that came over his face from behind, and a wave of sickening helplessness swept over me as I watched them both being dragged towards the door. I swung back to Nemo, but although he still held me tightly he was no longer looking at me. His head had jerked back and he was staring past them, and frowning at the sound which came floating up the stairs.

"Who is making that noise, Lee Sun?" He asked.

Flora had stopped struggling, and for an instant as the old man looked back at Nemo over the top of her head, our eyes met.

"New customer, Master. Very rich . . . very happy. Much singing."

"Too much disturbance, Lee Sun. Tell him to be quiet, or throw him out."

Lee Sun bowed, and as the door closed on them I heard the tune again, loud and clear.

"Up and down the City Road, in and out of the Eagle . . . That's the way the money goes . . . Pop goes the weasel . . ."

I stared down at the white fingers that still gripped my arm, and knew that whatever happened I mustn't look up at him, mustn't meet that glittering gaze. He was watching me, and waiting. I waited, too. His finger nails had a yellowish tinge, but the bones of his knuckles were white, whiter than the skin that was stretched over them, and beyond his cuff and the edge of his sleeve was the table cloth with the walnut shell still scattered on it, and the letter tucked half under the dish.

"Look at me," he said quietly. "There is no escape. Look up!"

"I'm not going to try and run away," I said, shaking my head.

"Good," he said, and I thought he was smiling. Gradually his hold loosened on me and his fingers slid away.

"I just want to know what you're going to do with me," I said, taking a step backwards and rubbing my arm.

"I have plans for you, William. Magnificent plans. At present you are a little afraid of me, but that will pass." He paused, and then his voice went on. "There is a bond between us now. You are not like the others, and you have proved to be an apt pupil. I like you . . . that is why I have decided to take you with me when I leave England – "

"No," I said, shaking my head. "No. You will never be able to put me under one of your spells again. I know what the secret is, and if I don't look at you, you have no power over me."

"But as time goes on you will have to look at me," he said, his voice gentle. "And you will see how well we shall get on together. It will be a just revenge for what Samuel has done to me. I have never had a son, but now I have you. Think of it, William, you and I, sailing the seven seas . . . and when we return home to China you will soon forget about the others."

"I shall never forget them," I said in a low voice. "And I would rather die than come with you."

"There is no escape," Nemo said, once again. "I have chosen you. You are mine now. And after a while," he went on, "when I am dead you will be rich, richer than you could ever imagine. All I have will be yours . . . and for me there will be the satisfaction of knowing that I have cheated Samuel for ever of what he treasures most. That chit of a girl as a kitchen maid, and you as my son. That shall be my reward."

I felt his power reaching out to me as he spoke, so that it was hard to tear my mind away from his. I tried not to listen, and strained my ears for the sound of the tune . . . Up and down the City Road . . . But he was speaking again.

"All these years he has been on my mind, day and night, no rest. It is because of him that I have had to spend my life on the other side of the world, and all for what? A simple mistake, that was all. I couldn't help the boy's death. I didn't know that they would cut him to pieces like that . . . no, no, mustn't think about it. It's over now, and I am within sight of my goal. This latest shipment has made me a rich man. I have the money already, and by tomorrow night I shall have the book."

I frowned. Somewhere beyond his voice I thought I could hear footsteps coming up the stairs. I looked at Nemo, but his glittering gaze was turned towards the window as though he could see something a long way off.

"He wrote it all down, you see. Every night in the tent, after the last bugle had sounded and before he went to sleep. Everything. He told me so before he died. 'It's all in the book, Nemo,' he said. 'Don't you forget that. And you won't be able to rest until you've found it, will you? They will get you in the end.'"

I watched him, remembering the faded sepia tints of the photograph I had seen in Samuel's desk . . . Samuel, Nemo and two other men. Suddenly he laughed, locking his fingers together and bringing his hands down on the table with a crash.

"Well I have found the book. It's taken me fifteen years, but I've found it. By tomorrow night it will be mine, and after that there will be nothing more to fear. And you, William . . ." He stopped, and his head jerked towards the door. I could hear it quite clearly now, just outside, and I straightened my shoulders and looked him full in the face.

"Half a pound of tuppeny rice, half a pound of treacle . . ." then Lee Sun's voice said:

"No, no. Not allowed in there . . . better to use other rooms."

"On the contrary, my friend, this is precisely the room that I want to go into, and since you are the owner of this house you had better come with me." For a moment a look of disbelief crossed Nemo's face, and then the door swung open.

"Samuel," I cried, as he appeared, pushing Lee Sun in front of him.

"Yes, dear boy, and in the nick of time I fancy. Are you all right?" He gave me a swift, loving look and smiled in his sunniest way.

"Yes," I said. "But the others . . . Flora and Dick."

"Don't worry, we'll have you all out of here in a trice, I promise, but let's not alarm the household just yet." As he spoke he kicked the door shut behind him and tightened his hold on Lee Sun. "Will you stop struggling, old man," he went on, in a pleasant voice. "You may be able to bully defenceless children, but you'll find that I'm stronger than you and if you don't keep still I'll crack your bones for you."

"Master!" Lee Sun screeched, his voice quavering.

"Be quiet," Nemo ordered him. "Well, Samuel, this is a surprise."

"Really?" Samuel murmured, raising his eyebrows. "I understood that you were looking for me. I came as quickly as I could once I'd received the message, but I must say, Nemo, that you don't look very pleased to see me."

"Message?" Nemo snapped. "What message?"

"Oh, didn't they tell you? Quite ingenious, really. You should never underestimate children, you know."

Out of the corner of my eye I saw Nemo beginning to move backwards towards the desk.

"Samuel, take care," I cried. "He's got a gun."

But it was too late. Nemo had seized the revolver and was pointing it at Samuel.

"And you, old friend, should not underestimate me," he said. "Stay where you are. This is loaded."

"Dear me," Samuel murmured. "This isn't much of a welcome,

I must say. But you hardly intend to use that thing, do you Nemo? Noisy things, guns. They attract a lot of attention. But then you know that, don't you?" Nemo's glittering gaze rested on Samuel and he smiled unpleasantly.

"Did you really think that I would allow you to get away with this?" he asked. "Release the old man." As he spoke he clicked back the safety catch on the revolver. Samuel watched him for a moment, and then relaxed his grip on Lee Sun. "Good," Nemo smiled. "Now it is your turn to be tied up." He signalled to Lee Sun, and I watched helplessly as the old Chinaman began to bind Samuel's wrists.

"Now the boy," Nemo said, when Lee Sun had finished. "Hands and feet."

"Is that really necessary?" Samuel asked. "He can't very well run away when you're pointing a revolver at him." Nemo's lips curled back in a contemptuous sneer.

"What a fool you are, Samuel, and as sentimental and womanish as ever, I see. You were unwise to come here and try to rescue them, but I am glad to have seen you one last time before I leave England for ever."

"How flattering," Samuel murmured. "Of course, there's nothing quite like the society of old friends, is there?" He smiled pleasantly. "Well, Nemo, now that you have us trussed up like Christmas turkeys, what do you mean to do next? No doubt you have something suitable planned. Not that I want to rush you, but I have the feeling that some more people may arrive to join the party before long. A few new faces would liven things up, don't you think?" He half turned his head towards the door as he spoke, and I saw Nemo stiffen and a look of fear flickered suddenly across Lee Sun's face.

"Is this a trick?" Nemo snapped.

"Oh no," Samuel replied, lightly. "Not at all. Opium smuggling, as I don't need to remind you, is a serious offence. Almost as serious as high treason, Nemo. Half the police force of Limehouse should be here at any moment."

Lee Sun gave a kind of gargle and started towards the door.

"Stay where you are," Nemo told him, swinging the revolver round. Then he turned his glittering gaze back to Samuel. "These tricks are exactly what I would expect from an itinerant conjuror," he sneered. "But they are futile. Seeing you just once more, and knowing that I have cheated you of all that you hold most dear has given me great pleasure." He smiled, and I saw him pick the letter up from the table and put it into his breast pocket. "Your friends, when they get here . . . if they get here, will find me gone. And the boy with me."

"Really?" Samuel's eyebrows shot up. "You mean to take William? Now that is a novel idea. I should warn you that he has some really shocking habits. Talks with his mouth full, ties his boot laces into knots, that sort of thing. You'll probably be tempted to drop him into the sea before you're out of Dover Harbour . . ."

At that moment I heard a whistle blow, and the sound of voices from downstairs.

"It sounds as though my friends have already arrived," Samuel murmured. "I fancy one of your people must have let them in. Really, you can't trust anyone nowadays, can you? And by the way," he went on, watching Nemo who had suddenly turned very white, "I should leave William behind. He won't be able to run very fast with his feet tied together, and I doubt whether you have time to attend to that now. A quick exit is what's required, my dear fellow."

Nemo's gaze flickered from Samuel to me and I saw the revolver tremble in his hands. He began to back towards the door which led into the next room.

"Master . . ." Lee Sun screeched, staring wildly at the door.

"Don't move, or I'll shoot you," Nemo told him.

Then several things happened very fast. Nemo was through the door that led to the inner room. It closed behind him, and we heard a thump and the crash of breaking glass. There were shouts coming from downstairs, and the next moment Lee Sun had bolted. We heard the door slam shut behind him and the thud of his footsteps outside.

"Samuel!" I shouted. "Look!"

From the inner room I saw a thin curl of smoke creeping under the door.

"Confound the man!" Samuel exclaimed. "He must have smashed the lamp and hopes to burn us alive. Well, we'll see about that. Roll off that chair, dear boy, and get over to the door while I see about these knots. Let's hope that our young friend has the wit to bring the police up here quickly. It appears that he doesn't much care for Nemo either, and I see his point. Itinerant conjuror, indeed!" As he spoke he was twisting and tensing his arms. "Did I ever tell you about the week I played the Hippodrome, Liverpool," he went on, quite calmly. "There was a fellow on the bill with me by the name of Houdini . . . escape artist . . . wouldn't tell me how he managed to get out of a tank of water when he was trussed up with ropes and chains, but I used to watch him every night from the wings. I must say, though, that old man ties a fine knot . . ."

"Hurry," I cried. "Oh do hurry, Samuel. I can smell burning."

Smoke was wreathing across the carpet by then, making me cough and splutter. With a final effort I rolled myself over to the door and banged against it with both feet.

"There! Done it!" I heard Samuel exclaim. Over my shoulder I could just see through the smoke that he had got his hands free. But the flames were licking under the door and the carpet was already alight. It was hard to breathe now.

"Hurry!" I moaned as a great wall of smoke billowed across the room towards me. "Hurry!"

Then the door was flung open and I saw the young Chinese man framed against the light.

"Thank you, my friend," I heard Samuel gasp as he appeared through the cloud and picked me up in his arms. "You are just in time to save us from being kippered alive, I fancy."

The next moment we were outside on the landing and heading for the stairs.

"He got away," I muttered. "After all that – " Samuel's arms tightened around me.

"I don't think we've quite seen the last of Nemo yet," he murmured. "But for the present all that matters is that he didn't take you with him."

Suddenly there seemed to be a great many policemen, and we were being pushed out through the front door and into the street.

"Flora," I cried. "And Dick . . ."

"Quite safe," Samuel said. "Thanks to our young friend. And now, dear boy, I think it's high time that we all went home."

CHAPTER THIRTEEN

In which Chang re-appears, and the mystery is unravelled . . .

And so it was that Flora, Dick and I came to be sitting with Samuel and his sister, Gus, at our own kitchen table in Kennington the next morning over a late breakfast of sausages and bacon.

Samuel had taken us straight home from Limehouse the day before, and put us all to bed, and after everything that had happened I suppose it wasn't surprising that we had slept the clock round and not woken up until the following morning. By that time Gus had arrived from Cornwall and had taken charge of the household. I should explain that her name is really Augusta, but because it's such a mouthful she's always been called Gus, and if adopted children can be said to have aunts, then Gus is our favourite aunt.

"When I think what these poor children have been through, and what might have happened to them," she said with a shudder, after there had been a pause in the conversation, "it makes my blood run cold."

"Yes, it was rather dreadful," Flora said, looking up from the piece of toast which she was spreading thickly with marmalade. "I think the worst thing of all was not knowing where Samuel was."

"And even Dick wouldn't tell us that," I nodded. "Although we guessed in the end . . ." I broke off, suddenly feeling ashamed all over again at the way I had so nearly given everything away to Nemo. Dick must have understood, because he leant across the table.

"It wasn't yer fault," he said.

"Of course it wasn't," Flora said. I shook my head, trying to forget his terrible, glittering gaze.

"It was a very good thing that Dick was with you," Samuel said, putting his hand on my shoulder. "Thanks to him managing to hide the doves, and whichever of you it was who had the bright idea of releasing them, I was able to reach Limehouse before it was too late. Whose idea was it, by the way?"

"That was Dick," Flora said. "But it was William who found the shaft."

"And you who crawled up into it," I said.

"Pluckiest thing I ever seen," Dick nodded approvingly.

"Oh I don't know," Flora said, looking modestly down at her plate.

I saw Samuel look at Gus, and for a moment a line appeared between his brows.

"I can't tell you what a relief it was when I saw the doves come in and found your message," he said. "At least then I knew where you were and could begin to make plans. It's thanks to all of you," he went on, "that we've finally succeeded in closing down the most notorious opium den in London. Of course I didn't intend that you two should be involved at all, and if I'd had any idea of the danger – "

"Don't say no more, Guvnor," Dick cut in, his voice low. "After all, 'ere we all are, safe and sound and no 'arm done."

"You knew it was an opium den, didn't you?" I said, looking across at him. Dick nodded.

"Oh yes, Dick knew all right," Samuel murmured. "He had as good a reason as anyone for wanting Nemo out of the way. That's why I asked him to help."

"And at least there's some now as won't go the way my old man did," Dick said, staring down at the table cloth. "Couldn't leave the stuff alone," he went on after a moment. "In the end it done for 'im, and now me and Emily's left ter look after me muvver."

"Emily?" Flora frowned. "The little girl in the bookshop?"

"She's me sister," Dick nodded. "And if it weren't for the Guvnor 'ere, I reckon we'd both be in the workhouse by now."

Flora and I looked at one another.

"So would we," she said solemnly. "We still think about it sometimes, don't we, William?"

"Sometimes," I said gruffly. "But not often."

"Well you needn't think about it any more," Samuel said in his firmest tone. "Because none of you is going to the workhouse. Not ever."

"I should think not indeed," Gus exclaimed, looking quite shocked. "The very idea of it." She picked up the tea pot and went to put more boiling water into it.

"You could come and live with us," Flora said, still looking at Dick. "And Emily, too," she added. But Dick shook his head.

"And leave me muvver alone? I don't think that would answer ... but I'd like ter come and see yer sometimes," he added. "I could take yer both mudlarking if yer like ... down by the river. Yer get eels there, real whoppers."

"I'd like that," I nodded. "Once all this is over."

"But it is over," Flora said. "Isn't it, Samuel?"

There was silence for a moment and we all looked at Samuel. All at once I had the feeling that Nemo's shadow had reached out and touched us as we sat there round the table and I gave a shiver. He was still there, somewhere, I thought, glancing out of the window. Then Samuel put his hand on my shoulder.

"The bad part is over," he said. "I promise you that. There's nothing for you to worry about any more."

"You're sure, aren't you?" I muttered.

"Quite sure," Samuel answered.

"All the same," Flora frowned, "there are still things I don't understand. We don't even know how Nemo got away."

162

"I can tell you that," Samuel said. "He had an escape route all planned, and a very crafty one it was, too. He went out through the window in the back room, and into one of the laundry baskets that was waiting down below. His Chinese workers spirited him away, and by the time the police arrived there was no trace of him."

"They found the opium though, didn't they?" I asked.

"Oh yes," Samuel nodded. "There wasn't time to hide that. Even accounting for the two baskets that you were hidden in I counted as many as twenty being unloaded from the wherrie, all filled with the stuff." He shook his head. "No wonder Nemo said it had made his fortune."

"Do you mean you were there?" Flora said. "Watching?"

"I arrived while you were still on board the wherrie," Samuel nodded. "Then I followed you to the house."

"So I did hear you whistling," I muttered. "I thought it was a dream."

"There are other things I don't understand," Flora went on after a moment. "The bookseller – "

"And the book," I cut in. "The book that Nemo wanted to buy . . ."

But Samuel was brushing the toast crumbs from his fingers.

"That story, along with all the others will have to wait for the moment," he said, standing up. "I must leave you for a while, but this time I promise to come back."

"You mean you're not going to tell us?" Flora exclaimed.

"Later, dear girl," he murmured. "Later. In the meantime I would like you all to stay here with Gus until I get back. And this evening," he went on, holding up his hand just as Flora was about to interrupt and looking round the table, "this evening we're going out together."

"You mean all of us?" Flora asked. Samuel nodded. "But where?"

"I'm afraid I can't tell you that either at the moment," he replied, smiling mysteriously. "Except to say that it's a rather special outing, so you had better put on your best bib and tucker."

"My new merino?" Flora cried, jumping up.

"And I shall be back at six o'clock, so make sure that you're ready." He kissed Gus on the forehead and waved goodbye to us, and we heard his footsteps go quickly up the stairs.

"He's gone," Flora exclaimed as the front door banged shut. "And just when I was going to ask him the most important thing of all."

"About Chang, you mean?" I said. She nodded.

"Chang?" Dick said, looking from one to the other of us. "Who's Chang?"

And for the life of me I couldn't tell whether he was serious.

Samuel had said that there wasn't anything to worry about any longer, but all the same Gus made sure that we stayed in the house for the rest of the day, and I realised that he wasn't taking any more chances when Flora came running back into the kitchen after a while to tell us that there was a policeman on duty outside the house. She was waving a letter about as she spoke, which had come by the second post, and as it was addressed to all of us, and was from Nellie, Gus said it would be all right to open it.

It was quite a short letter, but Nellie said that Rose was beginning to improve and that she had passed the crisis, whatever that was, and that she hoped we were all well and getting on all right without her. When we asked Gus about the crisis she looked serious and said that either you passed it, or you didn't, but if you did then you were well on the road to recovery, and Flora said that she was going to sit down there and then and write to Nellie to tell her everything that had happened.

"Do you think you should?" I said. "Even though we're safe she'll still worry, just knowing what's been going on."

Flora agreed that I was probably right. So she wrote quite a short letter instead, saying that Gus had come to stay and that we'd made a new friend, called Dick, and that Samuel was going to take us all out that evening on a surprise expedition and that she was going to wear her new merino; all of which was quite true. I added a post script to say that Dick was going to take us mudlarking and that we all missed her.

After lunch Gus stoked up the range and put a great many pans and kettles of water on to heat, because she had decided that baths and hair washing were in order after everything that had happened during the past three days.

"Like being fumigated when you've had scarlet fever," Flora said, and Gus laughed and said that was about it.

So I fetched the screen and the clothes horse, and we took it in turns to sit in the tin bath in front of the kitchen range while Gus went backwards and forwards with pan after pan of hot water. It took most of the afternoon, and by the time the last bath of dirty water had been emptied away it was five o'clock, and Gus and Flora disappeared upstairs where they spent the next hour prinking and tittivating.

Samuel was as good as his word, and he came running up the front steps as the clock struck six.

"Well I must say you all look a great deal better this evening," he smiled, surveying us as we stood together in the front hall. "I think you will do very nicely. And now – shall we go? The hansom is waiting."

"But where are we going to?" Flora asked. "We've waited all day to find out. Surely you're going to tell us now."

Samuel continued to look mysterious, though, as he swept us all out of the house and into the hansom.

The moon had risen and the sky was speckled with stars as we drove off along the Kennington Road, and over Westminster Bridge. It wasn't until we had passed Nelson's Column and were just turning into the Strand that Samuel announced that we must all be feeling rather peckish, and what about a spot of dinner.

"Is this it?" Flora asked, as we stoppeed outside a rather smart restaurant. "Is this the surprise?"

"Not entirely," he said. "But knowing you, dear girl, I'm sure you're ready for a little something."

It was more than a little something, as a matter of fact. We were conducted to a candle lit table at the far end of the restaurant, and handed menus so large that we could hardly hold them. They were all written in French, too, but it didn't matter because after a minute or two Samuel ordered lamb cutlets all round with plenty of gravy and mashed potato. After a while Dick nudged me and said that he felt a proper nob, sitting in a place like that, and what would his mother say if she could see him now. Then the lamb cutlets arrived, and when we'd all eaten as much as we could, finishing up with a chocolate and nut ice cream bombe, Samuel pulled out his half hunter and looked across at Gus.

"Well, if you're all ready," he said, "I think we should go. If we hurry we'll be just in time for the second half."

"Second 'alf of wot?" Dick asked, wiping the last of the ice cream from his mouth. "I don't think I can eat no more, Guvnor."

"I'm not surprised," Samuel smiled. "A little stroll is what's needed now, and that should get us there in perfect time. Shall we go?"

Flora and I looked at one another, and Gus smiled but said nothing, so I guessed that she knew where Samuel was taking us. It wasn't until we had been walking for ten minutes and were actually turning into Leicester Square that Flora and I realised.

"The Alhambra!" I exclaimed.

"Chang's first night," Flora cried. "But Samuel, I thought – "

"No questions," Samuel said. "Not yet. And remember, all of you, you must do exactly what I tell you. Be quiet, watch and listen."

"But why aren't we going in at the front?" Flora asked, taking his arm. "And why – ?"

"Dear girl," Samuel said, stopping and looking down at her. "I said no questions."

"I'm sorry," Flora said. "I forgot. I won't say another word."

"Good," he nodded. "There are surprises in store for all of you, but you must do as I tell you."

We had reached the stage door, and Fred was waiting for us.

"Am I glad to see you two safe and sound," he growled. "Fancy runnin' off like that. Still, all's well that ends well, and the artist turned up after all. Going very well, it is," he went on, turning to Samuel as he led us up the stone stairs. "Nearly brought the 'ouse down in the first 'alf. Curtain's just goin' up again." He pushed open the pass door which leads from the backstage world into the auditorium, and we found ourselves in a carpeted passage with doors leading into the stage boxes on our right. "This one's yours," he whispered. "Special like . . ."

The orchestra was already playing the overture for the second half and there was a rustling amongst the audience as they settled themselves in their seats after the interval. We barely had time to arrange ourselves on the chairs in the box when there was a roll of drums. Slowly, majestically, the red velvet curtains rose, and there, in the centre of the stage and standing in the beam of a single spotlight, stood Chang.

The audience applauded. Chang bowed and the lights came up, showing a black table, just behind him on which a number of things were arranged. To begin with he did some of the tricks which Samuel does, with scarves and handkerchieves until the whole stage seemed to be filled with brilliant fluttering colours. Then he piled all the scarves into a Chinese jar which stood on the table, and held up his white gloved hands so that the audience could see he had nothing in them. The next moment a red billiard ball had appeared from nowhere and was balanced between his finger and thumb. He gave a little flick, and there was another. Before long I counted ten red billiard balls appearing and disappearing between his fingers. Flora gave a little gasp, and I heard Dick suck in his cheeks. Even Samuel looked quite impressed, as he turned and murmured something to Gus.

As the applause died away, and the lights dimmed to a single spot, Chang stepped forward.

He stood just in front of the footlights, a solitary, dignified figure in his embroidered Chinese robe, waiting for the audience to settle into breathless silence. Only then did he speak.

"Ladies and gentlemen," he began, "which of you remembers from childhood the story of King Midas? He was the King who discovered that whatever he touched turned to gold. A talent, you might think, that any man might envy. But – " He held up one white gloved hand. "Mark what happened to him." There was a little pause. "One day," Chang continued, "the King sat in his castle. The sun came through the window as he sat there, thinking and twisting the ring of ebony wood which he always wore on his finger. Imagine the King's astonishment when he looked down and discovered that the ring had turned to gold." As he spoke Chang drew a small, black ring from his finger and held it up for the audience to see. Then, with a flick he turned it, and the ring had changed to gold. " 'This could be useful,' the King thought. 'My kingdom is short of money and we are in debt. Perhaps I could do this again. Perhaps I could turn my old, cheap watch into gold, too.' "

Chang held up a cheap looking fat turnip watch, flicked his wrist, and there was a gold half hunter, like the one that Samuel wears. The audience roared with delight.

" 'Well, this is all very fine,' the King said to himself, 'but suppose it's only the few things which I possess that it works on. I wonder for instance whether I could turn the Lord Chamberlain's watch into gold?' "

At this he paused for a moment to ask if anyone in the audience would like their watch turned to gold. A man in the front row held up a silver watch, and said that Chang would be welcome to try.

"You shall have it back, Honourable Sir, just as it is," Chang told him. Then he flicked his wrist again and held up another gold watch, and as the audience applauded he hooked it to a small line which hung along the front of the table, beside the first one.

"'Yes, my goodness, it's true,' King Midas thought, when he'd turned the Lord Chamberlain's watch to gold. 'Everything I touch turns to gold.' At this the King became very excited and went about touching everything he could see. His chairs and tables and plates and glasses and knives and forks."

As he spoke the lights rose and we saw a table set for dinner. Chang turned to the table and began to touch everything in turn, until the chairs and the plates, the cutlery and the glasses, even the table itself had been magically turned into gold which glinted and glowed in the light.

"The King went to his library next," he went on. "It was full of books. . . . Now does anyone in the audience happen to have a book with them?"

For a moment there was a breathless hush as he looked round at the faces turned towards him.

"Ah yes, thank you, Honourable Sir," At once the heads began to turn towards the stage box opposite ours, where a figure in the shadows was holding out a book. Chang went over and took it from him and placed it on the table. "Just an ordinary book, as you see?"

The sleeves of his figured silk robe passed over the book, just brushing it, and when he stepped back, there, sitting on the table was a book made entirely of gold.

"Wasn't that wonderful," Flora breathed beside me, as the audience gasped and there was another wave of applause.

I nodded, but my fingers were gripping the edges of the chair, and my eyes were drawn not towards the stage, but across to the box opposite ours where a dark figure sat, half hidden from view amongst the shadows.

"Soon the King was rich," Chang was saying, as the applause died away. "The richest man in the world. But he was also the loneliest man in the world. You see, nobody wanted to be near him, because everything he touched turned to gold. And as he grew richer he grew greedier, too. He touched his best friend, the man he'd known since childhood when they had played together in the palace gardens. Poor King Midas. Now he had all the gold he could ever want, but no friends. Ladies and gentlemen he had even turned his beloved daughter into gold. He wished that he could put the clock back; that he'd never discovered this terrible gift of his. But it was too late. And so the King left his palace and went out into the wilderness, where there was nothing to turn to gold except the rocks and stones, and there he was forced to wander until he died." The audience had grown very still.

"Back in the palace," Chang went on, "everything began to return to normal. The watches turned into ordinary silver watches again . . ."

Here Chang passed his hand over the two half hunters and with a smile handed the silver watch back to the man in the front row.

"And the plates and glasses and knives and forks, even the table and the chairs turned back to what they had been before." He passed his hand over the table and everything on it returned to normal. "Even the books in the library," he said, brushing his hand against the golden book on the table, and as he spoke drawing off the gloves that he had worn since the beginning of the performance. "Even the books turned back into ordinary books."

The book that lay on the table was no longer gold. Chang picked it up. And as he did so I saw the terrible livid scar which ran from his wrist to his index finger.

The figure in the box was leaning forward now, preparing to

receive the book. His hand was stretched out for it as Chang came towards him. He seized it greedily.

"Your book, Honourable Sir," Chang said.

Only then did he falter. His glittering gaze was turned towards the hand that was still held up in a final gesture towards him, the hand with the terrible scar on it. Chang bowed to him, with a little, mocking smile, before he turned again to the audience.

"The gold of the books and the chairs and the tables had all gone," he went on. "But nothing could bring back the King's best friend, or the King's beloved daughter."

As if in a dream I was aware that the curtain had begun to fall. I heard the audience thunder out their applause, and I saw the figure in the box opposite making for the door.

"Nemo!" Flora gasped.

"He'll get away," I muttered.

"No," Samuel said softly. "Not this time. Watch."

Then, as the curtain rose and fell and Chang bowed, we were aware of other figures in the box with Nemo, and before the lights came up in the auditorium he had been led away.

"You knew, didn't you?" Flora exclaimed, turning to Samuel. "You knew that he would be here . . ."

"That's what the letter was," I cut in. "The letter that the bookseller Mr Partridge, brought to the house. I remember seeing something sticking out of the corner of the envelope and wondering what it was. It was a theatre ticket . . ."

"Wot I wants ter know," Dick began. But at that moment Fred put his head round the door of our box.

"All ready for you, Mr Rolandson," he said. "Enjoy it, did you?" He went on, turning to us as Samuel picked up his silk muffler. "Nothing like a bit of magic, is there?"

"Nothing," Samuel agreed, smiling and taking Gus's arm as Fred winked broadly at us. "Come along all of you. It's time to go and congratulate Chang on a most accomplished performance. I hardly think I could have done better myself."

"Come in," said the voice from the other side of the door, and we followed Samuel into the dressing room.

"Please to be seated, Honourable friends," said Chang's voice from behind a screen in the far corner of the room. "I will be with you before the eye of the dragon has blinked twice. Well, how did you think that it went, Samuel?"

"Magnificent," Samuel replied, as Chang's figured silk robe was slung over the top of the screen. "Your best performance so far."

"Good of you to say so," Chang replied. There was a grunt and we heard him pouring water into a bowl. "I saw them take him away. . . . it all went exactly to plan."

"To perfection," Samuel agreed. There was a sound of splashing water and then a towel appeared beside the robe. Samuel glanced round at us. "Your admirers are all impatient to congratulate you," he smiled. "It's rather an invasion."

"If only all invasions could be such triumphant occasions, old fellow," Chang answered, in a way that suddenly sounded more English than Chinese. "I have the champagne all ready, and as soon as I've finished with this spirit gum I'll be with you."

Was it my imagination, I wondered, glancing at Flora. But she was inspecting the make up tray on the dressing table, and Dick was gazing at the two bottles of champagne which stood in an ice bucket by the door.

I saw him first reflected in the mirror as he stepped out from behind the screen, and I turned my head in astonishment as he came towards us.

"William, Flora," he said. "Dick . . . And, can it be? Can it truly be – Gus? After all these years! My goodness me, Samuel, what a very good looking sister you have."

He was amongst us, smiling down into our faces. Gus seemed

to know him. She took his hand and laughed. But he was a stranger. A man with silver streaked dark hair, in shirt sleeves and trousers and ordinary English braces.

Then Samuel put his arms round me and took Flora's hand and drew us towards the stranger with a smile.

"My dear fellow," he said, "do you realise that there are only two people in this dressing room who recognize you. I think, you know, that you have some explaining to do. Dick here thinks you're Mr Partridge, and William and Flora think you're Chang, which explains their quite unusual silence. It's only Gus and I who know your true identity."

The man laughed and held out his hand to all of us. As he shook my hand I saw the scar again.

"Allow me to introduce myself as I really am," he said. "My name is Forsyth, Harry Forsyth ... old friend and comrade in arms of Samuel here, and your most humble and obedient servant." He laughed again in a most delightful way, and turned to Samuel. "My word, you're right," he said. "They look as though they've been pole-axed, don't they? Make up, my dear young people. Make up. Look . . ."

He went over to the dressing table and began to pick things up.

"This is Mr Partridge's wig and beard, and here are his gold rimmed spectacles . . . Do you see now?"

As he spoke he put the spectacles on, his shoulders dropped and he stooped towards us like an old man, and there, in front of us, stood Mr Partridge.

"Blimey!" Dick muttered.

"All that's wanting is the beard, you see. . . . No doubt you've come for the Dickens first edition . . . But if you don't mind I won't put the beard on, since I've only just finished removing the spirit gum from Chang's wig and pigtail. But you get the general drift, I'm sure."

"That's why Chang disappeared," Flora gasped. "He really did, didn't he?"

"Yes, in order to become Mr Partridge."

"I really thought yer was an old codger," Dick muttered, shaking his head in bewilderment.

"I know you did. So did Emily. So did you, didn't you?" He added, turning to Flora and me. "It was bright of you to find that trap door. But I wish you'd waited."

"It was just as well they didn't," Samuel said. "I very much doubt whether we would have found the opium unless Nemo had kidnapped them."

"That's quite true," Harry Forsyth nodded. "We owe you a great deal, all three of you. Just the same," he went on, "I hate to think what was going through your minds when I turned up at the house as Mr Partridge and had my little talk with Nemo. You thought I'd betrayed you, didn't you?" We nodded. "I had to do it that way, just to make sure you were there. Dick, clever lad, had dropped his cap on the ground, so I guessed you must be next door. But I felt like a hound, knowing how frightened you all were. You couldn't guess Samuel was already in the house, of course, or that the police were on their way."

"He was going to turn me into a kitchen maid," Flora said with a shudder.

"And send me ter work in that laundry," Dick nodded.

"He had even more unpleasant plans for William," Samuel murmured. Gus shook her head.

"The wickedness of it," she said.

"I'm sorry we couldn't reach you before," Harry Forsyth said. "But it was the only way. You see, we knew that Nemo wanted that book more than anything else in the world, and with good reason. But we were pretty certain that he'd planned an escape route from the house, and we were right. If I hadn't come round there and dangled the bait of the book in front of him he'd have gone by now." He sighed. "It was a fearful risk, though. He might have recognised me, even though it's fifteen years since I last saw him. It was quite easy in the shop . . . I managed to keep in the shadows. But that room was rather too brightly lit and – "

"I know who you are," I gasped. "You're the man in the photograph. You, Samuel, Nemo and . . ."

"And my brother Tom," he said quietly. "You can't hide this, can you?" He went on after a moment, holding up his hand again so that we could all see the livid scar.

"That's why you wore gloves," I said. "And when you came to our house . . . I mean when Chang came to our house, you never took your hands out of your sleeves."

"You are observant," he smiled. "In the end this scar of mine turned the tables on Nemo, though. I knew that he would recognise it and understand that in the last resort we had outwitted him. When he looked down at me from the box his face was. . . ." He stopped. For a moment there was silence while he and Samuel looked at one another. Then he gave a little shiver. "Come on," he said. "I'm tired of being Chang, and Mr Partridge. Why don't we go back to your house and sit round the fire, and I'll tell you the whole story. We can take the champagne with us."

And so we all climbed into a brougham and drove back to Kennington. Now that Chang had become Harry Forsyth it seemed quite all right to be sitting downstairs in the kitchen instead of in the drawing room, and after Flora and Dick and I had drunk half a glass of champagne, which Samuel said was quite enough, and the grown ups had all drunk two glasses, Gus said she thought it was time we heard the whole story, and which of them was going to tell us.

"I think you should," Flora said, looking at Harry Forsyth. "Because it all began with you . . . or with Chang anyway. It began on Friday night, when you . . . I mean, Chang, came to the house."

"Yes," I nodded. "Flora's right."

"She's only partly right," Harry Forsyth said, leaning back in his chair and looking at Samuel. "As a matter of fact it all began long before that, didn't it, Samuel? About seventeen years ago, before you were born."

"Well go on then," I said. "Tell us from the beginning."

"Samuel, Nemo, Tom and I were all serving together in India at that time," he said after a moment. "We were sent to the north west frontier. That was how it began. Four friends, or so we thought, until we discovered that there was a traitor amongst us."

"Nemo," Flora nodded.

"Exactly. At that time the Russians were trying to get a foothold in northern India by backing the tribesmen who were fighting us. There was a great deal of money to be made by anyone who was prepared to give away the British positions and plans . . ."

"Give them away to the Russians, you mean?" I asked.

"Just so," he nodded. "We had mounted a small expedition to go up into the pass and try to root out some of the tribesmen. Nemo, Samuel, Tom and I were in the party. We got up into the pass all right, and all went well until one night Nemo disappeared. We didn't know what had happened to him. We thought he might have been captured by the tribesmen, and that wasn't a pleasant fate for anyone I can tell you. So Tom went off with a scouting party to try and find him." He paused and stared at the range for a moment. Then he went on. "That was when the tribesmen got him. Cut him to pieces, so we heard. And we never saw Nemo again, but we knew that he had betrayed Tom to the tribesmen."

"How did you know?" Flora asked.

"That's where the book comes in," Harry Forsyth said. "We didn't know it until after Tom's death, but he'd had his suspicions about Nemo for some time, and it was all written down in the diary he kept."

"Yer mean, 'e knew 'e was goin' ter be betrayed?" Dick asked.

"Not exactly, but he had a pretty shrewd idea that someone

would be. Nemo had been clever though. It was hard to get proper proof of what he was up to. Not until later, when it all came to light."

"And then it was too late," I said.

"Yes. Too late for Tom," Harry Forsyth said quietly.

"But how did Nemo know about the book?" Flora asked.

"Everyone knew about Tom's diary," Samuel smiled. "It was a standing joke amongst us, the way he used to write it every night after the last bugle had sounded."

"Nemo told me that, too," I murmured. "Just before you came into the room." Samuel turned to look at me.

"And Nemo was with Tom when he died," Harry Forsyth went on, after a moment. "We found that out later from one of the tribesmen we captured. When we discovered what Nemo had done we tried to find him, of course. To bring him back to justice. But he had vanished. It was then that Samuel and I vowed that one day we'd make sure he got his just desserts." Their eyes met across the table. "Well, it's taken a long time . . ."

"Fifteen years," Samuel nodded.

"But we caught up with him in the end."

It was quiet in the kitchen for a while. Gus stood up and put more coals on the range. Then she sat in Nellie's old armchair and Flora sat on the rug beside her.

"After that," Harry Forsyth went on, "Samuel left the army. I had already resigned my commission and begun the long search for Nemo. It was then that I caught cholera. I nearly died, and the rumour spread that I had not survived. I hoped that the rumour had reached Nemo, and I hit on the idea of a new identity. I became Chang, and I've been keeping track of Nemo ever since."

"All that time," Gus murmured. He nodded.

"First of all he went to Russia, and then down into China where he made his way to Shanghai. Before long he was engaged in the opium trade there. Samuel and I kept up a correspondence over the years, and bided our time. I went to America, to the west coast, where San Francisco was just opening up, and I began to work there as a magician while we waited. It was only this year that we discovered Nemo was planning to come to England with a consignment of opium, and then our plans matured. I put an advertisement in the Shanghai Times, to the effect that the diaries of Tom Forsyth had come to light, and gave a box number in London. And Nemo rose to the bait."

"He wrote to you?" I asked. Harry Forsyth nodded.

"The real Mr Partridge had just closed down his business and retired, which was useful, because we were able to take over his shop and Samuel worked from there until I arrived in England. It was vital, you see, that no suspicion of our plan should reach Nemo." He stopped and looked round at us. "That was why Dick was sworn to secrecy, and why Samuel shut you out of the drawing room the evening I arrived. We dared not run the risk of anyone finding out."

"We knew something was going on," Flora said. "Only we didn't know what it was."

"I dared not even tell Nellie," Samuel said. "Fortunately you were all going to The Cott next day. By the time you came back I expected the whole thing to be over. I certainly didn't want you mixed up in it."

"Only it all went wrong," Flora said.

"Yes," Samuel nodded. "Nemo found out where I lived . . . that's one reason why I went away, incidentally, to try and throw him off the scent. But his people must have been watching the house."

"I saw one of them," I nodded. "The night before we went to The Cott." Harry Forsyth and Samuel looked at one another. "I wanted to tell you the next morning," I went on. "Only there wasn't time. And then, when Flora and I were out one of them must have come in through the wash house window."

"That's the way we got in," Flora said. "I'm afraid we left it open."

"We knew because the photograph had gone," I said. "The one that was in your desk."

"I realised it had gone," Samuel said, after a moment. "Of course it wasn't really the photograph that Nemo was looking for." He glanced at Harry Forsyth. "It was Tom's diary. When he couldn't find it, or me, I suppose he must have hit on the idea of holding you two as hostages and trying to find out from you where I'd got to."

There was silence for a minute.

"I don't suppose the police will let him keep the diary, will they?" Flora said thoughtfully. "It wouldn't be right."

"You don't suppose I gave him the real diary, do you?" Harry Forsyth laughed. "That would have been the height of folly."

"But I saw you give it to him," Flora muttered. "We all did."

"It was a book, my dear old duffer. Just a book."

"Well, where is the real diary then?" I asked.

"In the vaults of my bank, where it's been for the past fifteen years," he said. "Come on," he went on, reaching for the champagne bottle, "let's have another glass all round, if Samuel will allow it. I want to drink a toast to you three. If you hadn't had the wit and the pluck to think of releasing those doves, Nemo might well have got away with it, instead of being safely tucked up in the police station out of harm's way. So here's to the three of you!"

"What will happen to him now?" I asked, when we'd finally finished the champagne.

"He'll have to stand trial, not only for opium smuggling, but also for his activities all those years ago," Samuel said. Harry Forsyth nodded.

"There are high ranking officers in the army who will be delighted to know that we've brought Nemo to justice," he said.

"The British army is like an elephant. It never forgets."

"And Tom is avenged at last," Samuel said.

Suddenly it really was all over. The coals shifted in the grate, Dick gave a mighty yawn, and Gus glanced up at the clock and announced that it was time for bed.

Samuel put his hand on my shoulder, and smiled at Dick, and Harry Forsyth picked Flora up and carried her towards the door.

"There was something I was going to ask you," she murmured sleepily. "About the pigtail. But I suppose it doesn't matter now."

"What will you do next?" Samuel asked. "After the season at the Alhambra ends?"

We all looked at the man who was Chang and Mr Partridge and Harry Forsyth.

"I'm going to be myself," he smiled.